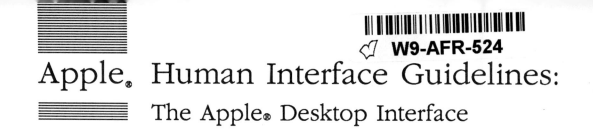

Apple® Human Interface Guidelines:

The Apple® Desktop Interface

Addison-Wesley Publishing Company, Inc.

Reading, Massachusetts   Menlo Park, California   New York   Don Mills,
Ontario Wokingham, England   Amsterdam   Bonn   Sydney   Singapore
Tokyo   Madrid   San Juan

Apple, the Apple logo, and LaserWriter are registered trademarks of Apple Computer, Inc.

Macintosh is a trademark of Apple Computer, Inc.

ITC Avant Garde Gothic, ITC Garamond, and ITC Zapf Dingbats are registered trademarks of International Typeface Corporation.

Microsoft is a registered trademark of Microsoft Corporation.

POSTSCRIPT is a trademark of Adobe Systems Incorporated.

Simultaneously published in the United States and Canada.

ISBN 0-201-17753-6
DEFGHIJ-DO-89
Fourth Printing, December 1988

Contents

Figures and tables

Foreword

From its inception, Apple Computer has had a vision: to bring the power and versatility of computers to ordinary people. The Desktop Interface, introduced with the Lisa® and further developed on the Macintosh™, represents a quantum leap toward that goal. This book presents the rationale behind the Apple Desktop Interface and provides guidelines for software developers who want their products to be consistent with the Desktop Interface. Various Apple® hardware systems can accommodate this interface in varying degrees. So far, the Macintosh is the most mature implementation of the interface, and we rely on it for the examples in this book. You'll understand this book better if you've used one or two standard Macintosh applications and read a Macintosh owner's guide.

The best time to familiarize yourself with the Desktop Interface is before beginning to design an application. Good application design happens when the developer has absorbed the spirit as well as the details of the Desktop Interface. Human interface design should come first, not last.

An interface is not merely a visual display—in fact, it's possible to have an interface with no visual display at all. A human interface is the sum of all communication between the computer and the user. It's what presents information to the user and accepts information from the user. It's what actually puts the computer's power into the user's hands.

One of the great advantages of the Desktop Interface is its consistency: a user who learns one application already knows a good deal about other applications. For example, Command-X and Command-V mean Cut and Paste in all standard applications; selecting a block of text and choosing Italic from the Style menu has the same effect in any application. This consistency makes it easier for a user to learn new applications; it also makes it less likely that a user who follows habits learned from one application will make a disastrous mistake when using a different one.

The Desktop Interface comprises features that are generally applicable to a variety of applications, but not all of the features are found in every application. In fact, some features are hypothetical because they *anticipate* future needs, and may not be found in any current applications.

This book will be most useful if you already have some experience with a desktop-based Finder program and with the concepts of pointing, clicking, and dragging with the mouse. You should also be familiar with some application programs that use windows, pull-down menus, and a mouse—preferably one each of a word processor, a spreadsheet or data base, and a graphics application.

Although you can find examples of most of the features described in this book by looking at existing applications, no one program has fully implemented these guidelines, and perhaps none ever will. Taken together, the Finder (version 5.5), MacWrite® (version 4.5), MacPaint® (version 1.5), and MacDraw® (version 1.9) come close to containing the full set of features as described here. Because these applications evolved in parallel with the Human Interface Guidelines, none of them is a perfect implementation of the guidelines: where the application differs from the guidelines, follow the guidelines. While there are some very good applications that deviate in significant respects from these guidelines, emulate those applications only with good reason. If you do deviate from the guidelines, make sure that the user will not get into trouble by following habits learned from standard applications: a pathological example would be to change the meaning of Command-S from Save to Shut Down-without-saving.

These guidelines are not the last word on this subject, just as the Desktop Interface is not the last interface. New features will be found that will make the interface more effective, and eventually new interfaces will appear. For now, these guidelines represent the interface that Apple recommends for all computers in the Apple II and Macintosh product lines.

You'll find detailed implementation specifications in the technical documentation for the particular Apple computer for which you're developing software. If you haven't already done so, you can become a registered or certified developer, which makes you eligible for additional information. Contact Apple Developer Relations for details.

This book is a joint effort of two groups at Apple: the Human Interface Group and the Technical Publications Group.

Chapter 1

Philosophy

The Apple Desktop Interface is the result of a great deal of concern with the human part of human-computer interaction. It has been designed explicitly to enhance the effectiveness of people. This approach has frequently been labeled *user friendly,* though *user centered* is probably more appropriate. It has been thought of as the ideal interface for beginners, though it would be more useful to think of it as good for people in general. It has been labeled *simple,* though *direct* and *effective* make more sense. And it has been described as *easy to learn,* though *accessible* would be as true.

A view of the user

Not very long ago, most users of personal computers were also programmers. In fact, many of them were computer builders as well, because personal computers were available only as kits. Today, most personal computers are seen as tools that magnify a person's ability to perform all kinds of tasks that were formerly done without computers. The Apple Desktop Interface provides a consistent and familiar computer environment in which people can perform their many tasks. People aren't trying to *use computers*—they're trying to get their jobs done.

Given this focus on people and their tasks, the Apple Desktop Interface has had to assume a model of people, in order to suit the interface to them. People, however, are delightfully complex and varied, which assures that a theory of human activity that would provide a complete framework for the design of human-computer interaction is a long way off. Such a theory would be oversimplified anyway, because computers themselves change the way we think, feel, and behave. Computer design and human activity must therefore evolve together. Apple believes that caring how people behave will help computer designers provide a consistent world that a person can enter with ease and effectiveness, even though many of the details of human activity are not understood.

The Apple Desktop Interface is based on the assumption that people are instinctively curious: they want to learn, and they learn best by active self-directed exploration of their environment. People strive to master their environment: they like to have a sense of control over what they are doing, to see and understand the results of their own actions. People are also skilled at manipulating symbolic representations: they love to communicate in verbal, visual, and gestural languages. Finally, people are both imaginative and artistic when they are provided with a comfortable context; they are most productive and effective when the environment in which they work and play is enjoyable and challenging.

The next section of this chapter sets forth ten human interface principles that explicitly emphasize the views expressed above. A subsequent section describes a programming strategy that takes these principles into account. Chapter 2 describes a specific set of elements for a Desktop Interface that can be used consistently across a range of very different applications. Chapter 3 provides standards and specifications for their implementation.

General design principles

This section describes the ten fundamental principles of the Apple Desktop Interface.

Metaphors from the real world

Use concrete metaphors and make them plain, so that users have a set of expectations to apply to computer environments.

Whenever appropriate, use audio and visual effects that support the metaphor.

Most people now using computers don't have years of experience with several different computer systems. What they do have is years of direct experience with their immediate world. To take advantage of this prior experience, computer designers frequently use metaphors for computer processes that correspond to the everyday world that people are comfortable with.

The desktop itself is the primary metaphor for the Apple Desktop Interface. It *appears* to be a surface on which users can keep tools and documents. Yet many of the elements of the Apple Desktop Interface don't have a clear physical counterpart. For example, scroll bars clearly belong to the computer domain; they only loosely resemble real scrolls. And pull-down menus aren't much like real restaurant menus, except in providing the opportunity to make choices from alternatives.

The desktop, then, is an inviting metaphor that provides easy access to the system. Other metaphors, especially when consistent with the desktop, can fit into the system. Once immersed in the desktop metaphor, users can adapt readily to loose connections with physical situations—the metaphor need not be taken to its logical extremes.

Direct manipulation

Users want to feel that they are in charge of the computer's activities.

People expect their physical actions to have physical results, and they want their tools to provide feedback. For example, when character keys are pressed, users like to hear a click as they see the corresponding characters appear on the screen. When a drawing tool is moved, a line appears. This is true whether or not a computer is being used. Moving a document from one folder or disk to another, or into the trash, can seem to be a physical activity with physical feedback in the computer world as it is in the paper world. The physical activity of moving the mouse reinforces the sense of an action with a real result.

Users want topics of interest to be highlighted. They want to see what functions are available at any given moment. If grave consequences might follow from any of those functions, they want to know about them—before any damage is done. They want clues that tell them that a particular command is being carried out, or, if it cannot be carried out, they want to know why not and what they can do instead.

People appreciate visual effects, such as animation, that show that a requested action is being carried out. This is why, when a window is closed, it appears to shrink into a folder or icon. Visual effects can also add entertainment and excitement to programs that might otherwise seem dull. Why shouldn't using a computer be fun?

See-and-point (instead of remember-and-type)

Users select actions from alternatives presented on the screen.

The general form of user actions is noun-then-verb, or "Hey, you—do this."

Users rely on recognition, not recall; they shouldn't have to remember anything the computer already knows.

Most programmers have no trouble working with a command-line interface that requires memorization and Boolean logic. The average user is not a programmer.

The Apple Desktop Interface is visually and spatially oriented. The way everything— text, applications, documents, lines, controls—appears on the screen is consistent and well thought out. The screen provides an environment in which people can work effectively, taking full advantage of the power of the computer while enjoying a sensible human environment.

Users interact directly with the screen, choosing objects and activities they are interested in by pointing at them. The mouse is currently the most common pointing device, but other effective pointing devices are available.

There are two fundamental paradigms for how the Apple Desktop Interface works. They share two basic assumptions: that users can see, on the screen, what they're doing; and that they can point at what they see. In one paradigm, users first select an object of interest (the noun) and then select an action (the verb) to be performed on the object. All actions available for the selected object are listed in the menus, so that users who are unsure of what to do next can quickly jog their memory by scanning through them. Users can choose, at any time, any available action, without having to remember any particular command or name. This paradigm requires only recognition, rather than recall, of the desired activities.

In the second paradigm, the user drags an object (the noun) onto some other object which has an action (the verb) associated with it. In the Finder, for example, the user can drag icons into the trash can, into folders, or into disks. No action is chosen from the menus, but it's obvious what happens to the object that is sent to another object. For example, an object sent to the trash can is discarded, and the document sent to a disk icon is copied to that disk. In this variant of the Desktop Interface, users do have to remember what an object such as the trash can is for, so it is especially important that objects look like what they do. If the trash can didn't *look* like the place to discard something, or we didn't know from daily experience that folders contain documents, such an interface wouldn't work. However, when this type of interface is well thought out, it can be easier to learn than menu commands.

Command-line interfaces, on the other hand, require the user to remember a command and type it into the computer. This kind of interface makes considerable demands on the user's memory—especially when the commands are complex or cryptic. Such an interface is especially galling to the new or infrequent user, but it distracts all users from their task and focuses attention instead on the computer's needs.

There are, however, some advantages to the *remember-and-type* approach. Sometimes, when the user is completely certain of what action is desired, a simple keystroke command may be the fastest way to achieve it. For this reason, some desktop applications include *keyboard equivalents* for some menu activities. Keyboard equivalents are a logical extension of the Apple Desktop Interface, fine-tuning it for particular situations. It is essential, however, that keyboard equivalents offer an *alternative* to the see-and-point approach—not a substitute for it. Users who are new to a particular application, or who are looking for potential actions in a confused moment, must always have the option of finding a desired object or action on the screen.

Consistency

Effective applications are both consistent within themselves and consistent with one another.

Having learned, in one application, a general set of skills, the user can transfer those skills to other applications. By using the standard elements of the Apple Desktop Interface, you ensure consistency within your application and you benefit from consistency across applications.

Within an application, there should always be one coherent way for the user to implement actions. Though some shortcuts may be provided, users should always be able to rely on familiar and straightforward ways to get things done.

The standard elements of the Apple Desktop Interface ensure consistency, ease of learning, and familiarity across applications. This benefits the typical user, who usually divides working time among several applications, and it benefits every software developer because the user learning how to use a new application builds on prior experiences with the same elements in other applications. This sometimes means that a programmer's new solution that precisely matches a particular situation should be set aside in favor of a slightly less effective but more commonly used solution. In most cases, consistency should be valued above idiosyncratic cleverness.

WYSIWYG (what you see is what you get)

There should be no secrets from the user, no abstract commands that only promise future results.

There should be no significant difference between what the user sees on the screen and what eventually gets printed.

A very important use of computers is the processing and printing of text and graphics. In some systems, the computer is an intermediary: the user manipulates a range of computer commands to indicate what is desired, and the computer passes these commands along to a printer. This kind of system keeps the user unnecessarily distant from the final document. The user should be in charge of both the content and the formatting (spatial layout as well as font choices) of the document. The computer should quickly and directly display the result of the user's choices, so the user doesn't have to wait for a printout or make mental calculations of how the screen version will be translated onto paper.

The principle behind this approach is known as *what you see is what you get* (abbreviated WYSIWYG, pronounced *wizzy-wig*). This approach is highly consistent with the direct manipulation aspect of the Apple Desktop Interface. For example, when a user uses the Finder to copy a document from one disk to another, the user "sees" a copy of the document move to the new disk and can trust that the document is now found on both disks. WYSIWYG is also in the spirit of using a computer as a thinking tool *and* as a production tool.

User control

The user, not the computer, initiates and controls all actions.

People learn best when they're actively engaged. Too often, however, the computer acts and the user merely reacts within a limited set of options. In other instances, the computer "takes care" of the user, offering only those alternatives that are judged "good" for the user or that "protect" the user from detailed deliberations.

On the surface, the concept of computer as protector may seem quite appealing, but this approach puts the computer, rather than the user, in the driving role—something quite at odds with the basic philosophy of the Apple Desktop Interface.

In the Apple Desktop Interface, if the user attempts something risky, the computer provides a warning, but allows the action to proceed if the user confirms that this is what he wants. This approach "protects" the beginner but allows the user to remain in control.

Feedback and dialog

Keep the user informed.

Provide immediate feedback.

User activities should be simple at any moment, though they may be complex taken together.

To be in charge, the user must be informed. When, for example, the user initiates an operation, immediate feedback confirms that the operation is being carried out, and (eventually) that it's finished. When the application isn't responding to user input because it's processing a different task, the user must be informed of when to expect delays, why, and for how long.

The user must also be kept informed of the progress of an operation: for example, the reason an operation can't be completed at a certain time as well as the fact that it can't.

This communication should be brief, direct, and expressed in the user's vocabulary rather than the programmer's.

Forgiveness

Users make mistakes; forgive them.

The user's actions are generally reversible—let users know about any that aren't.

Even though users like to have full documentation with their software, they don't like to read manuals (do you?). They would rather figure out how something works in the same way they learned to do things when they were children: by exploration, with lots of action and lots of feedback.

As a result, users sometimes make mistakes or explore a bit further than they really wanted to. Make your application tolerant and forgiving. Forgiveness means letting users do anything reasonable, letting them know they won't break anything, always warning them when they're entering risky territory, then allowing them either to back away gracefully or to plunge ahead, knowing exactly what the consequences are. Even actions that aren't particularly risky should be reversible. Tell the users about any exceptions to this rule.

When options are presented clearly and feedback is appropriate and timely, learning is relatively error-free. Alert messages should therefore be infrequent. If the user is subjected to a barrage of alert messages, something is wrong with the program design.

Perceived stability

Users feel comfortable in a computer environment that remains understandable and familiar rather than changing randomly.

People use computers because computers are versatile and fast. Computers can calculate, revise, display, and record many kinds of information far faster than people can. If users are to cope with the complexity that the computer handles so easily, they need some stable reference points.

To provide a visual sense of stability, the Apple Desktop Interface provides a two-dimensional space on which objects are placed. It also defines a number of consistent graphic elements (menu bar, window border, and so on) to maintain the illusion of stability.

To provide a conceptual sense of stability, the interface provides a clear finite set of objects and a clear finite set of actions to perform on those objects. Even when particular actions are unavailable, they are not eliminated from a display, but are merely dimmed.

It is the *illusion* of stability that is important, not stability in any strict physical sense. The environment can, and should, change as users interact with it, but users should feel that they have a number of familiar "landmarks" to count on.

Aesthetic integrity

Visually confusing or unattractive displays detract from the effectiveness of human-computer interactions.

Different "things" look different on the screen.

Users should be able to control the superficial appearance of their computer workplaces—to display their own style and individuality.

Messes are acceptable only if the user makes them—applications aren't allowed this freedom.

In traditional applications, the visual appearance of the screen has been a low priority and consequently somewhat arbitrary. In contrast, the Apple Desktop Interface *depends on* the visual appearance of the screen. People deserve and appreciate attractive surroundings. Consistent visual communication is very powerful in delivering complex messages and opportunities simply, subtly, and directly.

Users should have some control over the look of their workspaces. This allows individual expression and relieves the computer designer of having to devise one "look" that appeals to everyone.

The next section summarizes some basic principles of visual design.

Principles of graphic communication

Good design must communicate, not just dazzle. It must inform, not just impress.

The services of a skilled graphic designer are worth the expense.

The real point of graphic design, which comprises both pictures and text, is clear communication. In the Apple Desktop Interface, everything the user sees and manipulates on the screen is graphic. As much as possible, all commands, features, and parameters of an application, and all the user's data, appear as graphic objects on the screen.

Graphics are not merely cosmetic. When they are clear and consistent, they contribute greatly to ease of learning, communication, and understanding. The success of graphic design is measured in terms of the user's satisfaction and success in understanding the interface.

If you design your icons and other graphics on the target screen, rather than on paper, you'll take advantage of whatever that screen has to offer and you'll have the best design possible. Not all screens are alike. For example, a Macintosh Plus has approximately square pixels that are either black or white. Apple II pixels aren't square, and can be any of many different colors.

Visual consistency

The purpose of visual consistency is to construct a *believable environment* for users. Because such concepts as storing documents in folders and throwing things away in the trash can are the same both in the real world and in the Apple Desktop environment, users don't have to relearn them to begin working. This transfer of skills is one of the most important benefits of a consistent interface, especially for beginning users.

Photographic realism isn't essential; the important thing is that the user understands the intended meaning. A well-designed symbol or caricature can convey meaning better than a completely realistic picture.

If images don't efficiently convey meaning, the user is lost in an environment of random objects, and communcation breaks down. Graphics—the icons, windows, dialog boxes, and so on—are the basis of effective human-computer dialog and must be designed with that in mind.

Simplicity

Simple design is good design. Don't clutter the screen with too many windows, overload the user with complex icons, or put dozens of buttons in a dialog box. Because icons and dialog boxes must fit in a small space, the messages they convey must be simple and straightforward. Simple designs are easy to learn and to use, and they give the interface a consistent look.

The icons, menus, windows, and other graphic elements on the screen make up a basic language with which the user and computer communicate. The user selects an icon and chooses an action from a menu, effectively telling the computer to "Open MacPaint," for example. For this language to work well, the messages must be simple.

Clarity

Good graphic design begins with an understanding of the situation the user is in or of the problem being solved. A picture isn't always the answer—sometimes words do the job better. Make graphics clear and readable. Try them out on real users, not just on your fellow artists or programmers. The most important part of the graphic should be recognized first, then the second most important part, and so on. Use visual cues such as arrows, movement, and the arrangement of elements to direct the eye to the correct place. The symbols used in different kinds of alerts tell the user if the alert is a note, caution, or warning.

Animation, *when used sparingly,* is one of the best ways to draw the user's attention to a particular place on the screen. For example, users soon learn that the quickest way to find a pointer on a busy screen is to move the mouse, making the pointer move on the screen. Animated pointers reassure the user, during a lengthy process such as saving a large document to disk, that the system is alive and well.

A strategy for programming

The Apple Desktop Interface relies on some distinctive models for programming, some of which are unfamiliar even to experienced programmers.

To help the programmer make use of this interface, and to carry through in these models, some Apple hardware systems provide an abundance of tools in ROM. The developer derives two major advantages from using ROM-based tools and resources: compatibility and efficiency. The more a program bypasses or replaces these tools and resources, the more likely that sooner or later it will be incompatible with new products or features.

Although a developer might know a more direct way of getting information or performing an operation, using system-provided features ensures hardware independence. For example, always reference the proper data structures to determine the current size of a screen rather than using the constant values for current hardware.

The next sections deal with some important programming issues that are at the heart of the Apple Desktop Interface.

Modelessness

With few exceptions, a given action on the user's part should always have the same result, irrespective of past activities.

Modes are contexts in which a user action is interpreted differently than the same action would be interpreted in another context. In other words, the same action, when completed in two different modes, results in two different reactions. A mode typically restricts the operations that the user can perform while the mode is in effect.

Because people don't usually operate modally in real life, dealing with modes in computer environments gives the impression that computers are unnatural and unfriendly.

A mode is especially confusing when the user enters it unintentionally. When this happens, familiar objects and commands may take on unexpected meanings and the user's habitual actions cause unexpected results.

Most conventional software uses modes heavily. It's tempting to use modes because they sometimes make programming easier. But if you yield to the temptation too frequently, users will consider using your application a chore rather than a satisfying experience.

This is not to say that you should never use modes in applications. Sometimes a mode is the best way out of a particular problem. Most of these acceptable modes fall into one of the following categories:

☐ Long-term modes, such as doing word processing as opposed to graphics editing. In this sense, each application is a mode.

☐ Short-term "spring-loaded" modes, in which the user must constantly do something to maintain the mode. Examples would be holding down the mouse button to scroll text or holding down the Shift key to extend a text selection.

☐ Alert modes, in which the user must rectify an unusual situation before proceeding. Keep these modes to a minimum.

Other modes are acceptable if they do one of the following:

☐ They emulate a familiar real-life situation that is itself modal. For example, choosing different tools in a graphics application resembles the real-life choice of physical drawing tools. MacPaint and other palette-based applications exemplify this use of modes.

☐ They change only the attributes of something, but not its behavior. The boldface and underline modes of text entry are examples.

☐ They block most other normal operations of the system to emphasize the modality, as in error conditions incurable through software (for example, a dialog box that disables all menu items except Close).

If an application uses modes, there must be a clear visual indication of the current mode, and the indicator should be near the object most affected by the mode. A good example is the changing pointer in MacPaint: it looks like a pencil, paintbrush, spray can, or eraser, depending on the function ("mode") the user has chosen. It should also be very easy to get into or out of the mode (such as by clicking on a different palette symbol).

No mode should ever prevent a user from saving a document or quitting the application.

The event loop

Applications are prepared for the user to do anything at any time.

The event loop is central to programming for the Apple Desktop Interface. The event loop is the central routine of any application. An application doesn't have to expect a certain set of events in a particular order, but constantly looks for inputs (mouse actions, keystrokes, disk insertions) that can occur in any order and to which it must respond in specific ways.

This approach to programming contrasts with programs that systematically limit the alternatives available to the user, assuring that the user follows the "right" path to the "right" place. Instead, the emphasis is on responding to each local request the user makes, leaving the responsibility for the final destination with the user. In each context, the widest possible range of user activities should be allowed. For example, there's no reason not to let the user set printing options before there's anything to print.

Reversible actions

Always provide a way out.

Because the Apple Desktop Interface encourages users to be active, they often request something they don't really want. To encourage such deliberate (though often unplanned) activities and to give users a sense of control over these activities, programmers should make actions reversible whenever possible. Users should, for example, be able to cancel activities easily, particularly those that are unexpectedly involved. They should also have a range of deliberate choices to confirm that they do want to do something particularly drastic, complex, or time-consuming.

The screen

The screen is the stage for human-computer interactions.

In many computer systems, most of the activity is invisible. Users make inputs, to which the computer returns elaborate responses after some amount of calculation. The screen then becomes the "mail slot" through which exchanges between the user and the computer system take place.

In the Apple Desktop Interface, the screen displays a representation of the "world" that the computer creates for the user. On this screen is played out the full range of human-computer interactions. Initially, it provides the alternatives; then it reflects the results of requested activities; then it again shows the alternatives; and so on. And it does this in an extremely well-defined way. The details are in Chapters 2 and 3.

Though the screen is itself not the interface—the functionality provided by the interface elements is the interface—the screen does play a central role, and managing it is one of the programmer's most important tasks.

Plain language

Communicate with the user in concise and simple terms.

The Apple Desktop Interface is approachable by the unsophisticated user. It requires no special "language." In fact, much of the user-computer interaction is graphic. The user points to objects on the screen and selects from available lists; the computer changes text and graphics at the user's request.

Occasionally, the computer must display textual messages, either to describe a particular situation or to ask the user for a specific decision. In these instances, the phrasing must be very direct and unambiguous. It should inform users directly of the options available.

Whenever words are involved, the design team should include a skilled writer.

User testing

The primary test of the user interface is its success with users.

Can users understand what to do and can they accomplish the task at hand easily and efficiently? The best way to answer these questions is to put them to the users.

The design process

Users should be involved early in the design process so that changes in the basic concept of the product can still be made, if necessary. While there's a natural tendency to wait for a good working prototype before showing the product to anyone, this is too late for the user to have a significant impact on design. In the absence of working code, you can show test subjects alternate designs on paper or storyboards. There are many ways that early concepts can be tested on potential users of a product. Then, as the design progresses, the testing can become more refined and can focus on screen designs and specific features of the interface.

Test subjects

There is no such thing as a "typical user." You should, however, be able to identify some people who are familiar with the *task* your application supports but are unfamiliar with the specific *technology* you are using. These "naive experts" make good subjects because they don't have to be taught what the application is for, they are probably already motivated to use it, and they know what they need to accomplish the task.

You don't need to test a lot of people. The best procedure for formative testing (testing during the design process) is to collect data from a few subjects, analyze the results, and apply them as appropriate. Then, identify new questions that arise and questions that still need answers, and begin all over again—it is an iterative process.

Procedures

Planning and carrying out a true experimental test takes time and expert training. But many of the questions you may have about your design do not require such a rigid approach. Furthermore, the computer and application already provide a controlled setting from which objective data can be gathered quite reliably. The major requirements are

☐ to make *objective* observations

☐ to record the data *during the user-product interaction*

Objective observations include measurements of time, frequencies, error rates, and so forth. The simple and direct recording of what someone does and says while working is also an objective observation, however, and is often very useful to designers. Test subjects can be encouraged to talk as they work, describing what they are doing or trying to do, what they expect to happen, and so on. This record of a person's "thinking aloud" is called a *protocol* by researchers in the fields of cognition and problem-solving, and is a major source of their data.

The process of testing described here involves the application designer and the test subjects in a regular cycle of feedback and revision. Although the test procedures themselves may be informal, user testing of the concepts and features of the interface should be a regular, integral part of the design process.

Designing for disabled people

Computers hold tremendous promise for people with many kinds of disabilities. In terms of increasing productivity and mobility, computers can have a far greater impact on disabled people than on other users. But too often, computers become obstacles rather than enablers, because many disabilities make it hard to use standard computers and software. In most cases, thoughtful hardware design is the solution, but there are things that software designers can do, too.

Many of the modifications that make programs easier for disabled people to use are simple and inexpensive to make, and they often have a welcome and unexpected side effect—the programs are easier for *everyone* to use. Although sidewalk curb cuts are designed to help people who rely on crutches or wheelchairs, they are used and appreciated almost as much by skateboarders and stroller-pushers.

This section describes some of the ways you can design with disabled users in mind. For more information, contact Apple's Office of Special Education Programs.

Vision disabilities

People with vision problems have the most trouble with the output display. The ability of the Macintosh to handle different sizes of text makes it easy to accommodate the needs of many people with vision problems. Software can be designed with a "zoom" feature that automatically increases the size of characters on the screen.

Color is a problem for many people. Don't let people's ability to use your software depend on their ability to distinguish one color from another. Be sure that all information conveyed by color coding is also presented in some other way (by text, position, or highlighting).

Many people have difficulty using the instruction manuals that usually accompany software products, either because they have difficulty reading small print or because they physically can't handle books. These people appreciate having at least the most important part of the manual's text available in electronic form, so that they can display or print it in oversize characters, print it with a Braille printer, or have it read to them through a speech synthesizer. All users benefit from manuals in electronic form, which can quickly be searched for specific topics and keywords.

Hearing disabilities

Hearing problems are generally no obstacle to using computers, except when important cues are given only with sound. Aside from the obvious exceptions of music or voice-synthesis applications, software should never rely solely on sound to provide important information. Supplement all audible messages with visual cues, or allow the user to choose visible instead of audible messages.

Other disabilities

People with cognitive or verbal impairments are greatly helped by clear and simple language, icons with obvious meanings, and carefully designed displays. Don't make the user's success depend on his or her ability to *remember* many different things.

Another way to make computers easier for both disabled people and others is to provide macros, making it possible to combine a number of keystrokes and mouse movements into *one* keystroke. The way macros are created and accessed must be clear and simple. It shouldn't be easy for a user to invoke a macro accidentally.

Chapter 2

Elements of the Desktop Interface

To implement the principles stated in Chapter 1, Apple has defined two classes of standard interface elements for the Apple Desktop Interface:

☐ screen elements that define the "look" of the Apple Desktop Interface

☐ conventions for human-computer interactions that account for the "feel" of the interface

The consistent "look and feel" of this interface makes users feel comfortable when they use a range of applications on Apple computers.

Both kinds of elements are introduced briefly in this chapter. Chapter 3 provides details of their content and form.

Screen elements

The "look" of the screen provides a basic visual context for consistent use across applications.

Apple has paid a great deal of design attention to the visual integrity of the screen used in its Desktop Interface, to make this screen approachable and usable as a representation of available activities.

There are three fundamental screen elements: the **desktop, windows,** and **menus.**

The desktop

The desktop (shown in Figure 2-1) establishes the metaphor for the entire interface, and provides a stable, personalized background for the user. It's the "surface" that the user sees when a system is started up, and is the launching pad for all activities.

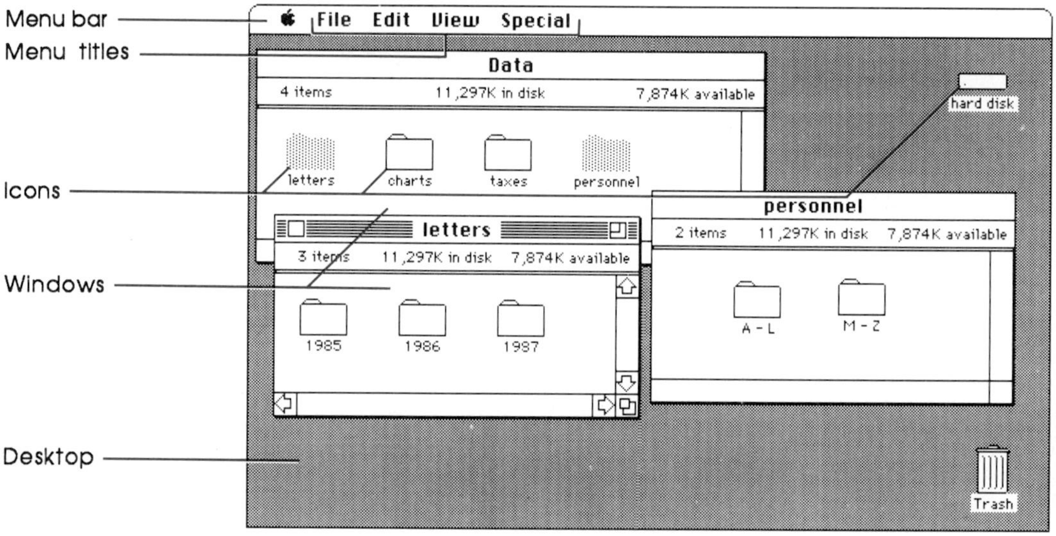

Figure 2-1
The Finder desktop

Visually, the desktop appears as a gray background on which objects are placed. The desktop can be personalized. The background has a default pattern, but the user can change its visual texture with the Control Panel desk accessory. The user also controls the location of objects on this desktop, and the size of some of them.

Icons, small pictures representing available objects, sit directly on the desktop. To select a disk, folder, application, or document, the user selects the corresponding icon, rather than having to type the name of the object it represents.

When a disk icon is selected, it can be opened to become a window, which also appears to rest on the desktop. The window presents a surface of its own, where the user sees icons representing the folders, documents, and applications that the disk contains. The user can open a number of disk windows on the desktop, and view their contents simultaneously.

The **Finder** is the application that controls the desktop, provides a view of available documents and applications, and lets the user organize, copy, move, rename, and delete them. The Finder also lets the user launch an application, which typically opens up its own window. An application is launched by opening either the application icon itself, or the icon for a document or stationery template created with that application.

Another desktop element is the **trash can,** represented by its own icon. The trash can icon is initially in the lower-right corner of the desktop, but can easily be moved. This element provides a very concrete way for users to delete documents and applications: they simply drag the corresponding icons into this trash can. Rather than mystifying the deletion of files, creating horrible images of computer memory losses, this mechanism provides a very understandable framework for this activity. It also prevents the user from inadvertently deleting materials with random keystrokes; putting something in the trash is a very deliberate and reversible action—up to a point, documents can be retrieved from the trash can.

Users can return to the desktop directly from any application. This provides a familiar environment where the user can organize past activities, perform housekeeping chores, and consider and initiate new activities.

Windows

A **window** is a frame for viewing something, as determined by the application. For example, each MacWrite window provides a view into a written document. To provide a *common* framework for the many kinds of information that users work with, windows are highly standardized (Figure 2-2).

Because more than one window can be viewed at once, users can arrange things the way they like and move information between windows. Because windows can overlap, users can "set aside" information yet still have ready access to it.

Manipulating windows—moving them, overlapping them, resizing them—does not affect the content of the windows, only the user's view of it. Again, this lets users tailor their work environment without fundamentally changing the elements in this environment.

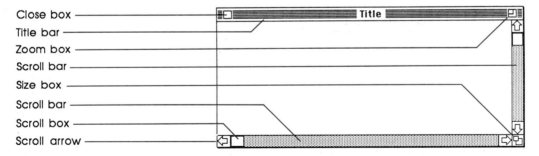

Figure 2-2
Standard document window

Window manipulation

There are very standard conventions for opening, closing, moving, sizing, scrolling, and zooming windows. No matter what application is being used, users know how to control the appearance of windows on the screen, and how to adjust the workspace for particular tasks and to their tastes.

When the user manipulates windows on the screen, visual feedback is immediate. When users move windows, they have the sense of directly moving them; changes in the graphic display keep up with the user's movements. When users open or close windows they see an illusion of such opening or closing, enhancing the sense of "real world" activity. When a document is scrolled, the scroll box provides direct visual feedback about the position of the current view within the document as a whole.

All of these mechanisms emphasize user control and the direct manipulation of concrete objects.

Dialog boxes, alert boxes, and controls

Among the other standard elements are window-like dialog boxes and alert boxes—and the specific controls that are used in these boxes. These boxes provide a standard framework in which the computer can present alternatives from which the user can choose.

The purpose of **dialog boxes** is to elicit responses from the user, typically several at one time. For example, the print dialog box allows the user to specify the number of copies to be printed, the pages to be printed, whether there should be a title page, and so on (Figure 2-3). A dialog box appears whenever the user chooses a menu item that is followed, in the menu itself, by an ellipsis (...). Standard dialog boxes suspend the system until the user either provides the needed information or cancels the operation.

All requests made in dialog boxes are phrased in plain language and in a friendly and nonthreatening manner.

When the dialog box is complete, the user dismisses it by "pushing a button" in the dialog box (by clicking the mouse button while the screen pointer is within a button-shaped object within the dialog box). This is not the same way standard windows are closed. Also unlike standard windows, modal dialog boxes can't be moved or resized.

```
┌─────────────────────────────────────────────┬──────────┐
│ ImageWriter                                  │    OK    │
│ Copies:[1]        Pages: ⊙ All  ○ From:[ ] To:[ ]  ├──────────┤
│                                              │  Cancel  │
│ Cover Page:    ⊙ No ○ First Page ○ Last Page ├──────────┤
│                                              │   Help   │
│ Paper Source:  ⊙ Paper Cassette  ○ Manual Feed └──────────┘
└─────────────────────────────────────────────┘
```

Figure 2-3
Dialog box

Alert boxes notify the user, in plain and polite language, whenever an unusual situation occurs (Figure 2-4). They can warn of dangerous situations, recommend corrective actions, or provide information that might change the user's plans—but the user is always in charge. There are different levels of alerts, according to the severity of the situation.

As with dialog boxes, users dismiss alert boxes by pushing a button, but can't move or resize them.

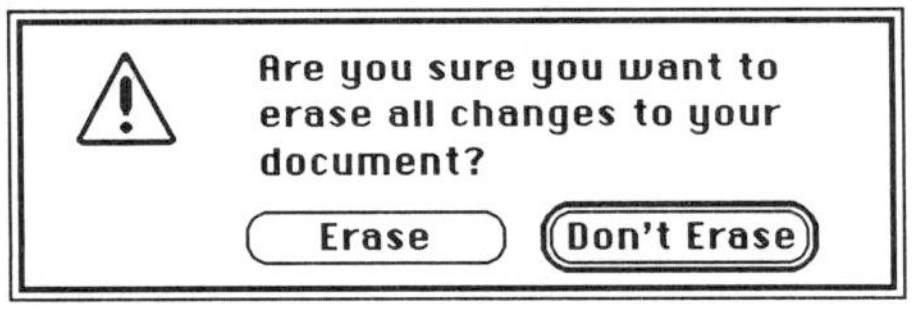

Figure 2-4
Alert box

Standard **controls** are used within dialog and alert boxes. Their appearance and functions are standardized. They provide users with familiar tools and formats for responding to the computer's need for information. Described in detail in Chapter 3, these controls include buttons, check boxes, radio buttons, and text entry fields.

Menus

Menus are central to the "noun-verb" principle of the Apple Desktop Interface: the user first selects an object (noun), either on the desktop or in a window, then chooses, from a menu, the operation (verb) to be applied to this object.

Because menus display the full range of potential activities available, users don't have to remember and type command names. Instead, they simply choose from the alternatives presented. The user's task is recognition, not recall.

Because they list all available activities, menus let users quickly get an overview (or, for new users, a preview) of what is possible at any given moment.

Finally, pull-down menus make it possible to keep unnecessary details out of sight, and out of the way of the main task, while still making those details quickly and easily available. The user "pulls down" a menu only when it's needed—the rest of the time, the menu is "rolled up" into the menu bar at the top of the screen.

The overall concept of pull-down menus comprises three fundamental screen elements: the menu bar, where the name of each available menu appears; pull-down menus, which appear only when the user wants them to; and the menu items themselves.

The menu bar

The **menu bar** serves as a stabilizing element. Even when the screen changes drastically, as when the user changes from one application to another, the menu bar is always visible at the top of the screen, adding to the illusion of stability amid a flexible environment.

The elements of the menu bar—the words and phrases that are the titles of the different menus—are also quite stable (Figure 2-5). Three of the menus—the Apple menu, the File menu, and the Edit menu—are **standard menus** that appear as the first three menus in almost every application. When making up your own menus, do not give them the same names as standard menus.

In addition to the three standard menus, each application has its own unique menus. Because they appear to the right of the more standard menus, application-specific menus don't interfere with the user's sense of stability.

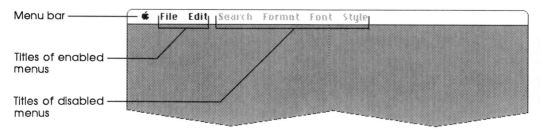

Figure 2-5
Menu bar

Menu items

Within an application, menu items don't usually vary (the exceptions are "integrated" applications in which, for example, the spreadsheet and the word processor may have different sets of menus). This consistency contributes to the user's sense of stability. Even though certain items are sometimes unavailable, they remain in the menu—dimmed to show that they're unavailable at the moment.

The user can either browse through menu items—without having to choose any of them—or choose one item to be executed. To browse, the user simply holds the mouse button down and moves the pointer through the menu bar, which pulls down one menu at a time.

Choosing a menu item is a deliberate process. To choose an item from the menu that's pulled down, the user drags the pointer down to that item and releases the mouse button.

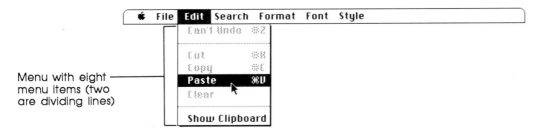

Figure 2-6
Menu

Menus can include a wide range of items, typically grouped by type to make the most sense to the user (Figure 2-6).

The **Apple menu,** often called the **desk accessory menu,** is always the leftmost menu (Figure 2-7). It lists the desk accessories that are currently installed on the system. This menu changes when the user installs a new desk accessory or deletes an old one. Desk accessories are usually "mini-applications," implemented as device drivers, that can operate at the same time as a full-scale application.

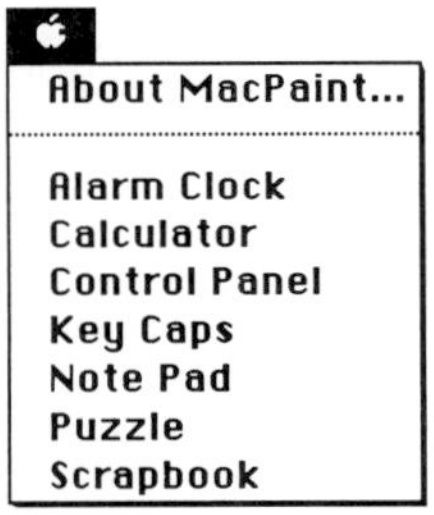

Figure 2-7
The Apple menu

The second menu is the **File menu,** which lets the user perform tasks relative to whole documents—opening, closing, saving, and printing—from within an application (Figure 2-8). A key item in the File menu is the **Quit** operation, which lets the user quit an application at any time. This is in contrast to traditional applications that require the user to step backward to a "Main Menu" before quitting.

What is color?

Color is made up of three elements:

- **Hue** is what is usually meant by "color": whether it's red, blue, green, or yellow, and so on.

- **Saturation** is the purity of a color—rich, intense colors are highly saturated; dull or diluted colors are not very saturated. For example, pink is a low-saturation red; navy blue is a high-saturation blue.

- **Brightness** is how light or dark a color is—how much white is in it. Some pure hues are naturally brighter than others: yellow is the lightest hue; violet is the darkest. Bright colors attract the eye.

Standard uses of color

In traditional user interface design, color is used to associate or separate objects and information in the following ways:

- ☐ discriminate between different areas
- ☐ show which things are functionally related
- ☐ show relationships among things
- ☐ identify crucial features

Color coding

Different colors have standard associations in different cultures. "Meanings" of colors usually have nothing to do with the wavelength of the color, but are learned through conditioning within a particular culture. Some of the most universal meanings for colors are:

- **Red:** Stop, error, or failure. (For disk drives, red also means disk access in progress; don't remove the disk or turn it off.)

- **Yellow:** Warning, caution, or delay.

- **Green:** Go, ready, or power on.

It's also generally true that reds, oranges, and yellows are perceived as hot or exciting colors, while blues and greens are cool, calm colors. Colors often have additional standard meanings within a particular discipline: in the financial world, red means loss and black means gain. To a mapmaker, green means wooded areas, blue means water, yellow means deserts. In an application for a specific field, you can take advantage of these meanings; in a general application, you should allow users to change the colors, and to turn off any color coding that you use as a default. Having more than one color coding scheme in effect at any one time can be very confusing.

For attracting the user's attention, orange and red are more effective than other colors, but usually connote "warning" or "danger." (Be aware, though, that in some cases, attracting the eye might not be what you want to do. For example, if "dangerous" menu items are colored red, the user's eye will be attracted to the red items, and the user might be *more* likely to select the items by mistake.)

Although the screen may be able to display 256 or more colors, the human eye can discriminate only about 128 pure hues. Furthermore, when colors are used to signify information, studies have shown that the mind can only effectively follow four to seven color assignments on a screen at once.

General principles of color design

Two principles should guide the design of your application: begin the design in black and white, and limit the use of color, especially in the application's use of the standard interface.

Design in black and white

You should design your application first in black and white. Color should be *supplementary*, providing extra information for those users who have color. Color shouldn't be the only thing that distinguishes two objects; there should always be other cues, such as shape, location, pattern, or sound. There are several reasons for this:

- **Monitors**: Many users won't have color monitors. The majority of Macintosh computers and many Apple II's have only a monochrome display.

- **Printing**: Currently, color printing is not very accurate, and even when high-quality color printing becomes available, there is usually a significant change in colors between media (as you've noticed if you've ever compared an art reproduction to the original).

- **Colorblindness**: A significant percentage of the population is colorblind to some degree (in Europe and America, about 8% of males and 0.5% of females have some sort of defective color vision). The most common form of colorblindness is an inability to distinguish red and green from gray. In another form, yellow, blue, and gray are indistinguishable.

- **Lighting**: Under dim lighting conditions, colors tend to wash out and become difficult for the eye to distinguish—the differences between colors must be greater, and the number of colors fewer, for them to be discernible. You can't know the conditions under which your application may be used.

Limit color use

In the *standard interface* part of applications (menus, window frames, and so on), color should be used minimally or not at all; the Desktop Interface is very successful in black and white. You want the user's attention focused on the content of the application, rather than distracted by color in the menus or scroll bars. Use of color in the *content area* of your application depends on what the application is for.

Graphics applications, which are concerned with the image itself, should take full advantage of the color capabilities of Color QuickDraw, letting the user choose from and modify as many colors as are available.

Other applications, which deal with the organization of information, should limit the use of color much more than this. Color coding should be allowed or provided to make the information clearer. Providing the user with a small initial selection of distinct colors—four to seven at most—with the capability of changing those available, or adding more, is the best solution.

Contrast and discrimination

Color adds another dimension to the array of possible contrasts, and care must be taken to maintain good readability and graphic clarity.

Colors on grays

Colors look best against a background of neutral gray. Colors within your application will stand out more if the background and surrounding areas (such as the window frame and menus) are black and white or gray.

Colored text

Reading and legibility studies in the print (paper) world show that colored text is harder to read than black text on a white background. This also appears to be true in the limited studies that have been done in the computer domain, although almost all these studies have looked at colors on a black background, rather than a white background. (Keep this in mind if you hear that "amber is the best color for text.")

Beware of blue

The most illegible color is light blue, which should be avoided for text, thin lines, and small shapes. Adjacent colors that differ only in the amount of blue should also be avoided. However, for things that you *want* to make unobtrusive, such as grid lines, blue is the perfect color (think of graph paper or lined paper).

Small objects

People cannot easily discriminate between small areas of color—to be able to tell what color an object is, that object must be large enough to see without effort. Changes in the color of small objects must be obvious, not subtle.

Specific recommendations

Remember that color should never be the only thing that distinguishes objects. Other cues such as shape, location, pattern, or sound should always be used in addition to color, for the reasons discussed above.

Backgrounds

Generally, all interface elements (menus, window frames, and so on) should maintain a white background, using color to replace only pixels that are black in the black-and-white interface. Maintaining the white background helps keep the clarity and the "look and feel" of the Desktop Interface.

Outlines

Outlines of menus, windows, and alert and dialog boxes should remain in black. Edges formed by color differences alone are hard for the eye to focus on, and these objects may appear against a colored desktop or window.

Highlighting and selection

Most things—menu items, icons, buttons, and so forth—should highlight by reversing the white background with the colored or black bits when selected. (For example, if the item is red on a white background, it should highlight to white on a red background.) However, if multiple colors of *text* appear together, Color TextEdit allows the user to set the highlighting bar color to something other than black to highlight the text better. The default for the bar color is always black.

Menus

In general, the only use of color in menus should be in menus used to choose colors. However, color could also be useful for directing the user's choices in training and tutorial materials: one color can lead the user through a lesson.

Windows

Since the focus of attention is on the content region of the window, color should be used only in that area. Using color in the scroll bars or title bar can simply distract the user. (The one exception is that if the user has color-coded icons in the Finder, the title of a window—not the whole title bar—may be the same color as the icon from which it came.)

Dialog and alert boxes

Except for dialog boxes used to select colors, there's no reason to color the controls or text in dialog boxes; they should be designed and laid out clearly enough that color isn't necessary to separate different sections or items. Alert boxes must be as clear as possible; color can add confusion instead of clarity. For example, if you tried to make things clearer by using red to mean dangerous and green to mean safe in the Erase Disk alert box, the OK button—"go"—would be *red* and the Cancel button—"stop"—would be *green*. Don't do this.

Pointers

The pointer should always be visible. Most of the time, when it's being used for selecting and choosing, it should remain black—color might not be visible over potentially different colored backgrounds, and wouldn't give the user any extra information. However, when the user is drawing or typing in color, the drawing or text-insertion pointer should appear in the color that is being used. Except for multicolored paintbrush pointers, the pointer shouldn't contain more than one color at once—it's hard for the eye to discriminate small areas of color.

Sound

The high-quality sound capabilities of some Apple computers let sound be integrated into the human interface to give users additional information. This section refers to sound as a part of the interface in standard applications, not to the way sound is used in an application that uses the sound itself as data, such as a music composition application.

When to use sound

There are two general ways that sound can be used in the interface:

☐ It can be **integrated** throughout the standard interface to help make the user aware of the state of the computer or application.

☐ It can be used to **alert** the user when something happens unexpectedly, in the background, or behind the user's back.

In general, when you would like to put an indicator on the screen to tell the user that something has occurred—for example, that mail has come in, or that a particular process has finished—this is a good time to use a sound.

Getting attention

If the computer is doing something time-consuming, and the user may have turned away from the screen, sound is a good way to let the user know that the process is finished, or it needs attention. (There should also be an indication on the screen, of course.)

Alerts

Common alerts can use sounds other than the SysBeep for their first stage or two before bringing up an alert box. For example, when the user tries to paste when there's nothing in the Clipboard, or tries to backspace past the top of a field, different sounds could alert them.

Modes

If your application has different states or modes, each one can have a particular sound when it is entered or exited. This can emphasize the current mode, and prevent confusion.

General guidelines

Although the use of sound in the Desktop Interface hasn't been investigated thoroughly, these are some general guidelines to keep in mind.

Restraint

Be thoughtful about where and how you use sound in an application. If you overuse sound, it won't add any meaning to the interface, and will probably just be annoying.

Redundancy

Sound should never be the only indication that something has happened; there should always be a visible indication on the screen, too, especially when the user needs to know what has occurred. The user may have all sound turned off, may have been out of hearing range of the computer, or may be hard of hearing.

Unobtrusiveness

Most sounds can be quite subtle and still getting their meaning across. Loud, harsh sounds can be offensive or intimidating. You should always use the sound yourself and test it on users for a significant period of time (a week or two, not twenty minutes) before including it in your application—if you turn it off after a day, chances are other people will, too. You should also avoid using tunes or jingles—more than two or three notes of a tune may become annoying or sound silly if heard very often.

Significant differences

Users can learn to recognize and discriminate between sounds, but different sounds should be significantly different. Nonmusicians often can't tell the difference between two similar notes or chords, especially when they're separated by a space of time.

User control

The user can change the volume of sounds, or turn sound off altogether, using the Control Panel desk accessory. You should remember this, and should never override this capability. Always store sounds as resources, so users can change sounds and add additional sounds.

Summary

The look and feel of the Apple Desktop Interface has been defined very carefully to make it approachable by both new and experienced computer users, and to let those users focus on their tasks rather than on the computer. This is accomplished with just a few basic objects (the desktop, windows, menus) and with a few basic actions (pointing, selecting, and keyboard input). This simplicity is key to delivering on the promise of effective human-computer interaction described in Chapter 1.

Chapter 3

Specifications

This chapter provides detailed specifications for the elements that were introduced in Chapter 2. If you follow these specifications and take advantage of standard ROM-based tools, your applications will be as compatible as possible with other applications for the same hardware.

Introduction

The active application controls all communication between the user and the computer. For your application to have the "look and feel" of the Apple Desktop Interface, it must include the standard interface elements.

The Finder is a program that lets the user launch applications and organize, copy, move, rename, and delete documents. When the user, from the Finder, opens an application or a document belonging to an application, that application becomes active and displays its document window. In a single-application environment, only one application can be active at a time, and it has control of all windows (except desk accessories). The user must return to the Finder to change from one application to another. Multiprocessing will eventually allow several applications to share the screen, each having control over its own windows, and the user will be able to switch applications directly.

Each document is a unified collection of information—a business letter, list, worksheet, chart, animation sequence, or piece of music. A complex application, such as a data base system, might require several related documents. Some documents can be processed by more than one application; but each document has a **principal application**, which is usually the one that created it. If other applications can process the same document, they are called the document's **secondary applications**. Opening a document, whether through a menu or by double-clicking its icon, launches the application that originally created that document (assuming the application is available).

The desktop

The primary unifying metaphor in the Apple Desktop Interface is the desktop itself, shown in Figure 3-1. It provides a sense of apparent stability, remaining constant while its content changes.

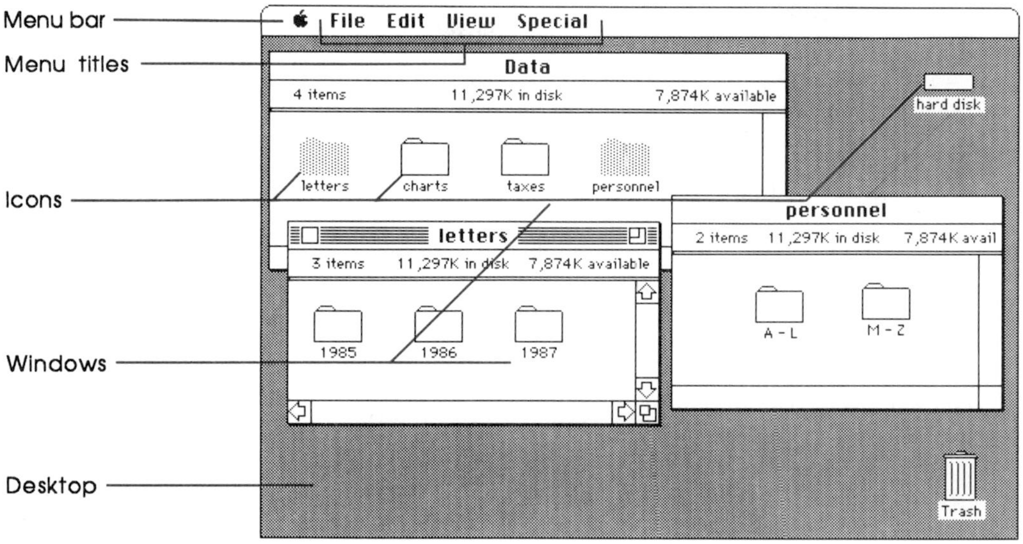

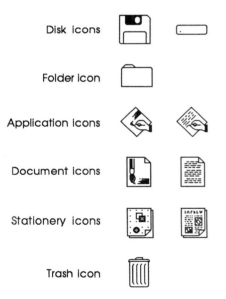

Figure 3-1
The Finder desktop

Desktop **icons** are graphic representations of such things as disks, folders, applications, documents, stationery, and the trash can, as shown in Figure 3-2.

Disk icons

Folder icon

Application icons

Document icons

Stationery icons

Trash icon

Figure 3-2
Six kinds of Finder icons

Applications are the programs with which users do their work or play—from word processors to music composers to spreadsheets. **Documents** are the user's data files—the place where all the work done in an application is stored. **Stationery** files are templates that can contain anything a regular document can contain: a memo or overhead template, or only page setup or layout information. **Folders** let the user organize the desktop; they can contain applications, documents, stationery templates, other folders, or any other sort of file. All of these objects can be stored on **disks**, and can be erased by dragging their icons to the **Trash** on the screen.

Icons contribute greatly to the clarity and attractiveness of an application. The use of icons in addition to (or instead of) words can also make it easier to translate programs into other languages, except where the icons have different meanings in different cultures. An item is easier to remember when it's represented by an icon with text than if it's represented by either an icon alone or text alone. Wherever an explanation or label is needed, consider using an icon.

The two basic subsystems of the desktop are the **windows** that allow flexible display of information, and the **menus** (including palettes) that make many operations immediately available.

Windows

The way the user accesses any document is through a window. A window is a view into the document—if the document is larger than the window, the window is a view of a portion of the document. The application puts one or more windows on the screen, each window showing a view of a document or of auxiliary information used in processing the document.

Generally, it is unwise to allow multiple windows for the same document because it confuses the relationship of windows to icons ("Which window do I close to close the document?"). If multiple views are desirable, the window can be split. (See the section "Splitting a Window.")

There are several kinds of windows. Standard document windows are the most obvious kind, but dialog and alert boxes are technically windows too. Most of this section deals with document windows. Controls, dialog boxes, and alert boxes are discussed together after the discussion of document windows.

This section is about a window's structural components, or window frame. For a standard document window, these components include the title bar, size box, close box, zoom box, and scroll bars. The application determines the *content* of the window.

Document windows

Because a document may contain more information than a window can display at one time, the window provides a view of a portion of a document. Document windows also provide a graphic representation of opening, closing, and other operations performed on documents. Windows are usually, but not necessarily, rectangles. Figure 3-3 shows a standard document window and its components.

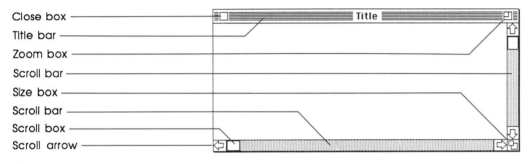

Close box
Title bar
Zoom box
Scroll bar
Size box
Scroll bar
Scroll box
Scroll arrow

Title

Figure 3-3
Standard document window

Opening and closing windows

Windows appear on the screen in different ways as appropriate to the purpose of the window. The application controls at least the initial size and placement of its windows.

A standard window has a **close box.** When the user clicks the close box, the window goes away. (In the Finder, this is animated—the window shrinks into the folder or icon from which it was opened.) If an application doesn't support closing a window with a close box, it shouldn't include a close box on the window.

The application in control of the window determines what's done with the window visually and logically when the close box is clicked. To the user's eye, a window, once closed, can seem either to retreat into an icon or to simply disappear. In reality, either the information in the window may be saved (this is the usual case) and will still be there when the window is reopened, or the changes are not saved and the window is empty each time it's reopened.

When closing a document, the user must be able to choose whether to save any changes made to the document since the last time it was saved.

Multiple windows

Some applications can keep several windows on the desktop at the same time. Each window is in a different plane. Windows can be moved around on the desktop much as pieces of paper can be moved around on a real desktop. Each window overlaps those behind it and is overlapped by those in front of it. Even when windows don't overlap, they retain their front-to-back ordering.

Each application may deal with the meaning and creation of multiple windows in its own way. Different windows can represent

☐ separate documents being viewed or edited simultaneously

☐ related parts of a logical whole (such as the listing, execution, and debugging of a program)

☐ different views of the same information (such as a spreadsheet and a graph that represent the same number

The disadvantage of multiple windows is that the desktop can become cluttered. Some applications provide, in the menu bar, a Windows menu. This menu allows the user to quickly choose a window even though it may be out of sight under other windows.

Figure 3-4 illustrates multiple windows.

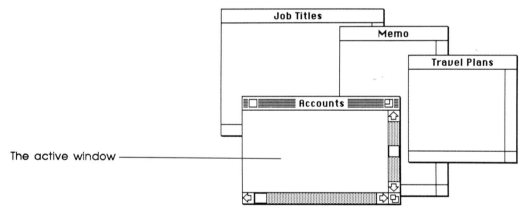

Figure 3-4
Multiple windows

The active window

Although several windows can be open on the desktop at the same time, the user can work in only one window at a time. This window is called the **active window.** All other open windows are **inactive.** Things can be happening to documents in inactive windows, but only the active window can be manipulated directly. For example, if the user chooses Close from the File menu, only the active window is closed.

To make a window active, the user clicks anywhere inside it. Making a window active has two immediate consequences:

□ The window changes its appearance: its title bar is striped and the scroll bars, close box, zoom box, and size box appear.

□ The window "moves" to the frontmost plane, so that parts that had been covered by other windows become visible.

Clicking in an inactive window activates it, but makes no other changes. To make a selection within the window, the user must click again. When the user clicks in a window that has been deactivated, the window should be reinstated just the way it was when it was deactivated, with the scroll box in the same position and the same selection highlighted.

When a window becomes inactive, the visual changes that took place when it was activated are reversed. The title bar is no longer striped and the scroll bars, close box, zoom box, and size box disappear. Although the information within the window remains visible (except where obscured by other windows), any selection is deselected. Figure 3-4 shows the visual difference between active and inactive windows.

Moving a window

Although each application has its own way of initially placing windows on the screen, the user can move an active window—to make more room on the desktop or to uncover a window it's overlapping—simply by dragging it by its title bar. A dotted outline of the window follows the pointer until the user releases the mouse button. At the release of the button the full window is redrawn in its new location. Moving a window doesn't affect the appearance of the icons or document within the window; they move right along with the window.

The act of moving an inactive window makes it active—unless the user holds down the Apple key while moving the inactive window, in which case the window moves, in the same plane, without becoming active.

The application should ensure that a window can never be moved completely off the screen.

Changing the size of a window

If a window has a **size box** in its lower-right corner, the user can change the size of the window—enlarging or reducing it to the desired size.

Dragging the size box attaches a dotted outline of the window to the pointer. The outline's upper-left corner stays fixed, while the lower-right corner follows the pointer. When the mouse button is released, the window is redrawn in the shape of the dotted outline.

If a window can be moved, but not resized, then the user ends up constantly moving windows on and off the screen. If the user moves the window off the right or bottom edge of the screen, the scroll bars are the first things to disappear. To scroll the window, the user must move the window back onto the screen again. If, on the other hand, the window can be resized, then the user can change its size instead of moving it off the screen, and will still be able to scroll.

Resizing a window doesn't change the position of the upper-left corner of the window or the appearance of the part of the view that's still showing; it changes only how much of the view is visible inside the window. One exception to this rule is a command such as Reduce to Fit (in MacDraw), which changes the scaling of the view to fit the size of the window. If, after choosing this command, the user resizes the window, the application changes the scaling of the view.

Applications determine the minimum and maximum window size, which should depend on the physical size of the display. If the user tries to shrink the window below its minimum size, the attempt is ignored.

Window zooming

The more open documents on a desktop, the more difficult it is for the user to locate, select, and resize the one to be worked on. Some Apple computers have a feature in ROM that allows users—with a single mouse click in the window's **zoom box**—to drag and size the active window to a size and location they previously selected, and then to return the window to full size with another click. Figures 3-5 and 3-6 show a window in the standard state and in the user-selected state.

If this feature is present, the zoom box is present at the right end of the window's title bar (Figure 3-5). Because window zooming is not available on all Apple computers, application programs must check the ROM and, if the feature is not present, bypass it. (Window zooming does not involve the variable magnification you get with a zoom lens.)

Application developers are encouraged to use the zoom window function on systems that make it available.

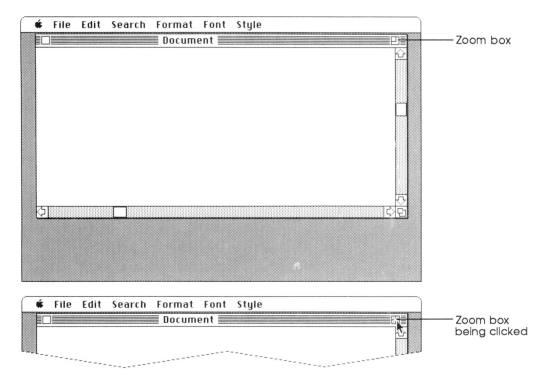

Zoom box

Zoom box
being clicked

Figure 3-5
Window in standard state

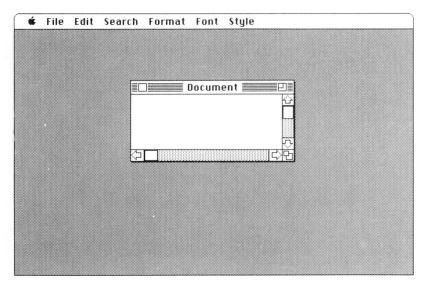

Figure 3-6
Window in user-selected state

The application supplies the values for the size and location of the standard state of the window as well as the initial values for the size and location of the user-selected state. The **standard state** is generally the full screen, or close to it, and should be the size and location best suited to working on the document. As often as they want, users can specify the **user-selected state** of the window, generally the size and location best suited to organizing the desktop so that documents can be found and selected.

The user can't change the standard size and location, but the application can change it within context. For example, a word processor might define the standard size and location as wide enough to display a document whose width is specified in the Page Setup dialog box. If the user invokes Page Setup to specify a wider or narrower document, the application might change the values for the standard size and location to reflect that change.

Explicit dragging or resizing of the window is handled according to these guidelines, regardless of the presence or absence of the zoom window feature. The effect of dragging or resizing depends on the state of the window and the degree of movement. In the Macintosh computer, the user must drag or resize a window at least seven pixels to cause a change in the user-selected state.

Windows open into the user-selected state if possible. The application must make sure that the user-selected state fits on the current screen: if the window was previously on an alternate or large screen, and is then opened on a single or smaller screen, the application changes its size and location so the entire window is visible.

Scroll bars

Scroll bars are used to change which part of a document is shown in a window. Only the active window can be scrolled.

A **scroll bar** is a light gray rectangle having on each end an arrow in a square box (Figure 3-7). A window can have either a vertical scroll bar or a horizontal scroll bar, or both. Vertical scroll bars are on the right side of the associated window; horizontal scroll bars run along the bottom of the window. Inside the scroll bar is a white rectangle called the **scroll box.** The rest of the scroll bar is the **gray area.**

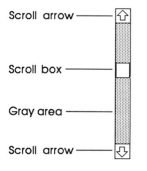

Scroll arrow

Scroll box

Gray area

Scroll arrow

Figure 3-7
Vertical scroll bar

A scroll bar represents one dimension (either top to bottom or left to right) of the entire document. The scroll box represents the relative location, in the whole document, of the portion currently visible in the window. The scroll box may also represent the relative amount of the document that can be seen in the window. (See "Proportional Scroll Boxes" later in this section.)

If the user "moves" the document by clicking either a scroll arrow or in the gray area, the scroll box moves along with it. If the user drags the scroll box, the document "moves" along with it. If the document is no larger than the window, the scroll bars are inactive (the scrolling apparatus isn't shown in them). If the document window is inactive, the scroll bars aren't shown at all.

There are several ways the user can move a document through the window: sequential scrolling with the scroll arrows, "paging" windowful by windowful through the document, and dragging the scroll box. These are described in the following sections. There is also the automatic scrolling that takes place when the user drags the pointer past the window boundary or types at the bottom of the window. To experience these firsthand, try them out in an application such as MacWrite.

Scrolling with the scroll arrows

Clicking or pressing one of the scroll arrows lets the user see more of the document in the direction of the scroll arrow, so the document seems to move in the opposite direction. For example, when the user clicks the top scroll arrow, the document moves down, bringing the top of the document into view. The scroll box moves in the direction of the arrow being clicked.

Each click in a scroll arrow causes movement a distance of one unit in the chosen direction, with the unit of distance being appropriate to the application: one line for a word processor, one row or column for a spreadsheet, and so on. For smooth scrolling, units within a document should always be the same size. Pressing the scroll arrow causes continuous movement in its direction.

Scrolling by windowful

Clicking the mouse anywhere in the gray area of the scroll bar advances the document by a windowful. The scroll box, and the document view, move toward the place where the user clicked. Clicking *below* the scroll box, for example, brings the user the next windowful toward the bottom of the document. Pressing in the gray area causes the display of consecutive windowfuls until the user releases the mouse button, or until the location of the scroll box catches up to the location of the pointer. Each windowful is the height or width of the window, minus one unit overlap (where a unit is the distance the view scrolls when the scroll arrow is clicked once), so that a little of the previous information is shown as a reference point. Vertical scrolling by windowful can also be done using function keys on some keyboards (see "Function Keys" for details).

Scrolling by dragging the scroll box

The scroll box shows the relative position, within the whole document, of the portion of the document visible in the window. (The position of the scroll box has nothing to do with the position of the pointer, which can be outside the window; or with the position of the insertion point, which can be anywhere in the document.) If the scroll box is halfway between the top and the bottom of the scroll bar, then the visible portion of the document is halfway between the top and the bottom of the document. To scroll the document, the user drags the scroll box. For example, to see the beginning of the document, the user drags the scroll box to the top of the scroll bar.

If the user starts dragging the scroll box, and then moves the pointer a certain distance outside the scroll bar, the scroll box stops following the pointer and snaps back to its original position. If the user then releases the mouse button, no scrolling occurs. But if the user, still holding down the mouse button, moves the pointer back *into* the scroll bar, the scroll box again begins to move up or down with the pointer.

If a document has a fixed size (as in MacDraw, for example), and the user scrolls to the right or bottom edge of the document, the application can display a light gray background between the edge of the document and the window frame.

Some applications put the page number inside the scroll box so that the user can see the page number change as the document scrolls.

Proportional scroll boxes

An interesting variation on scroll boxes is the proportional scroll box. Instead of being a constant size, it starts out (in an empty document) filling the full length of the vertical scroll bar, indicating that all of the document is visible in the window. Then, as content is added to the document, the scroll bar shrinks proportionally (though it never gets smaller than a minimum size). In other words, as the amount of the document that the user can't see grows, the scroll bar's gray area grows too.

Automatic scrolling

There are four instances when the application, rather than the user, scrolls the document. These instances involve some potentially sticky problems about how to position the document within the window after scrolling.

☐ When the user reaches the edge of the window while entering information into the document from the keyboard, scrolling happens automatically. The distance scrolled depends on the kind of application: one line in a word processor, one field in a data base or spreadsheet.

☐ When the user moves the pointer past the edge of the window while holding down the mouse button, the window keeps up with the selection by scrolling automatically in the direction the pointer has been moved. The rate of scrolling is the same as if the user were pressing on the corresponding scroll arrow or arrows.

☐ When the user performs an operation on a selection that isn't currently showing in the window, it's usually because the user has scrolled the document after making the selection. In this case, the application scrolls the window so that the selection is showing before performing the operation. This makes it clear to the user what is being changed.

☐ When the application performs an operation whose side effect is to make a new selection or move the insertion point, scrolling happens automatically. An example is a search operation, after which the object of the search is selected. If the new selection isn't already showing in the window, the application must scroll the document to show it. Another example: after a paste operation, the insertion point is after the end of whatever was pasted, which sometimes makes scrolling necessary.

The second and third cases present the same problem: where should the selection be positioned within the window after scrolling? The primary rule is that the application should avoid unnecessary automatic scrolling. Users prefer to retain control over the positioning of a document. The following guidelines should be helpful:

☐ If part of the new selection is already showing in the window, don't scroll at all. An exception to this rule occurs when the part of the selection that isn't showing is more important than the part that is showing.

☐ If scrolling in one orientation (either horizontal or vertical) is enough to reveal the selection, don't scroll in both orientations.

☐ If the application is scrolling to a selection that is smaller than the window, position the selection so that some of its context is showing on each side. It's better to put the selection somewhere near the middle of the window than right up against the corner.

☐ Even if the selection is too large to show in the window, it might be preferable to show some context rather than trying to fit as much as possible of the selection in the window.

Splitting a window

Sometimes users want to see (and work on) two separate parts of a document simultaneously. They can do this by splitting the window into independently scrollable **panes.**

Applications that support splitting a window into panes place **split bars** at the top of the vertical scroll bar or to the left of the horizontal one, or both (Figure 3-8). The user can drag the split bar anywhere along the scroll bar. Releasing the mouse button creates a new split bar at that location, splits the window there, and divides the appropriate scroll bar into separate scroll bars for each pane.

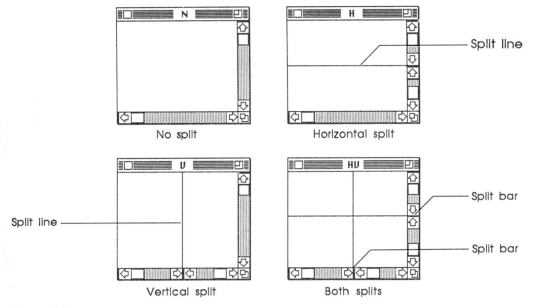

Figure 3-8
Types of split windows

After a split, there are separate scroll bars for each pane. The panes are still scrolled together in the orientation of the split, but can be scrolled independently in the other orientation. For example, if the split is vertical, then vertical scrolling (using the scroll bar along the right of the window) is still synchronous; horizontal scrolling is controlled separately for each pane, using the two scroll bars along the bottom of the window (Figure 3-9).

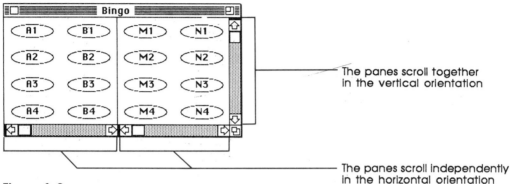

The panes scroll together in the vertical orientation

The panes scroll independently in the horizontal orientation

Figure 3-9
Scrolling a split window

If the application allows only one split (one vertical and/or one horizontal split), the split bar is moved to a new location along the scroll bar. If the application allows multiple splits, the original split bar remains at the top or left end of the scroll bar, and additional splits can be peeled off from it. To remove a split (to return the window to a single pane), the user drags the split bar back to the top or end of the scroll bar.

Even when there are several panes, there is still only one selection or one insertion point, which may appear in any number of the panes. If a change is made in one pane, the change is reflected in all panes where that portion of the document is visible. If the application has to scroll automatically to show the selection, the pane that should be scrolled is the last one the user clicked in. If the selection is already showing in one of the panes, no automatic scrolling takes place.

Panels

If the application divides a document window more or less permanently into different areas, each having a different content, these areas are called **panels.** Unlike panes, which show different parts of the same document but are functionally identical, panels are functionally different from each other but might show different interpretations of the same part of a document. For example, one panel might show a graphic version of a document while another panel shows a text version, or one panel might show a numeric representation of some data while another shows a graph based on the same data.

Panels, like windows, can have scroll bars and can be split into more than one pane. Whether to use panels instead of separate windows depends on the application. Multiple panels in the same window are more compact than separate windows, but they have to be opened, moved, and closed as a unit.

Controls, dialog boxes, and alerts

Selecting the single object of an operation and then choosing a menu command works well whenever operations are simple and act on only one object. For those times when a command requires more than one object or needs additional information before it can be executed, the Apple Desktop Interface includes

□ dialog boxes, to allow the user to provide the needed additional information before a command is executed

□ alerts, to notify the user whenever an unusual situation occurs

Because dialog and alert boxes often use controls, controls are described in this section, even though they're also used in other kinds of windows.

Most dialog and alert boxes should be centered in the upper third of the screen, whatever size screen they're displayed on. The exception to this is a dialog or alert box whose placement is linked to something else on the screen, such as a dialog box that appears with its default button in the same place as the menu item that brought up the dialog box, allowing the user to click the button without moving the mouse.

Controls

To enhance the user's sense of direct manipulation, many of an application's features can be implemented with **controls:** graphic objects that, when manipulated with the mouse, cause instant action with visible or audible results. Controls also can change settings to modify future actions.

There are many types of controls. Buttons, check boxes, radio buttons, and scroll bars are all available from the Macintosh Toolbox. You can also design your own controls, such as the thermometer and gauge shown in Figure 3-12.

Buttons

A **button** is a small screen object usually labeled with text (Figure 3-10). Clicking or pressing a button performs the action described by the button's label. Button labels should be unambiguous. Often, a label describing the *result* of pressing the button (Erase, Revert, or Don't Save, for example) is clearer than just Yes, No, or OK. If one button is the default button (that is, if pressing Return or Enter has the same result as pressing this button), then it is doubly outlined to distinguish it from the other buttons.

Buttons usually perform instantaneous actions, such as completing operations defined by a dialog box or acknowledging error messages. They can also perform continuous actions, in which case the effect of *pressing* on the button (rather than just clicking it) would be the same as the effect of clicking it repeatedly.

Two particular buttons, OK and Cancel, are especially important in dialog and alert boxes. They're discussed under "Dialog Boxes" and "Alerts" later in this chapter.

Default button

Figure 3-10
Buttons

Check boxes and radio buttons

Check boxes and radio buttons let the user choose among alternatives.

Check boxes act like toggle switches (comparable to the text attributes in the Style menu). Use check boxes to indicate the state of an option that must be either off or on. The option is on if the box is checked; otherwise it's off. The check boxes appearing together in a given context are independent of each other—any number of them can be off or on. In Figure 3-11, check boxes 1 and 2 are on; if a user clicked box 3, all three boxes would be on.

Radio buttons typically occur in groups. They're called radio buttons because they act like the buttons on a car radio. They're mutually exclusive—at any given time, exactly one button in the group is on. Clicking one button in a group turns off whichever button was on before. In Figure 3-11, radio button 2 is on; if a user clicked button 3, button 2 would go off.

If more than one group of buttons is visible at one time, the groups must be made distinct from one another.

Both check boxes and radio buttons are accompanied by text that identifies what each button does.

☒ Check Box 1   ○ Radio Button 1
☒ Check Box 2   ⦿ Radio Button 2
☐ Check Box 3   ○ Radio Button 3

Figure 3-11
Check boxes and radio buttons

Dials

A **dial** displays the value, magnitude, or position of something in the application or system (Figure 3-12). Some dials also allow the user to alter that value. Dials are predominantly analog devices, displaying their values graphically and sometimes allowing the user to change the value by dragging an **indicator.** Dials may also have a digital display.

The most common example of a dial is the scroll bar. The indicator of the scroll bar is the scroll box that represents the relative position of the window over the whole length of the document. The user can drag the scroll box to change that position.

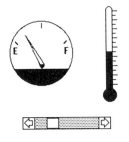

Figure 3-12
Dials

Dialog boxes

Commands in menus normaly act on only one object. If a command needs more information before it can be performed, it presents a **dialog box** to gather the additional information from the user. The user can tell which commands will use a dialog box to get more information because these commands are followed by an ellipsis (…) in the menu.

A dialog box is a rectangle that may contain text, controls, and icons. There should be some text in the box that indicates which command caused the dialog box to appear and what the function of the box is.

The user sets controls and fills text fields in the dialog box to provide the needed information. When the application puts up the dialog box, it should set the controls to some default setting and fill in the text fields with default values, if possible. One of the text fields (the "first" field) should be highlighted, so that the user can change its value just by typing in the new value. If all the text fields are blank, there should be an insertion point in the first field.

In general, dialog boxes should be laid out with the most important information and controls at the top left, working down to the less important information, ending with the default button—the button most likely to be clicked—at the lower right. In Western countries, people are used to reading and writing from left to right and top to bottom, so this is the most natural way to fill in information.

Editing text fields in a dialog box should conform to the guidelines detailed under "Editing Text" later in this chapter.

After editing an item, the user has two options:

☐ Pressing the Tab key accepts the changes made to the item and selects the next field in sequence.

☐ Clicking in another field accepts the changes made to the previous item and selects the newly clicked field.

Dialog boxes can be either modal or modeless.

A **modal dialog box** is one that the user must explicitly dismiss before doing anything else, such as making a selection outside the dialog box or choosing a command. Figure 3-13 shows an example of a modal dialog box.

Figure 3-13
A modal dialog box

Because it restricts the user's freedom of action, you should use this type of dialog box sparingly. In particular, the user can't choose a menu item while a modal dialog box is up and therefore can do only the simplest kinds of text editing. For these reasons, the main use of a modal dialog box is when it's important for the user to complete an operation before doing anything else.

A modal dialog box usually has at least two buttons: OK and Cancel. OK dismisses the dialog box and performs the original command according to the information provided. It can be given a more descriptive name than Yes or OK: "Start printing," for example. Cancel dismisses the dialog box and cancels the original command. It should always be called Cancel.

A dialog box can have other kinds of buttons as well. These may or may not dismiss the dialog box. The **default button** (the most likely choice in the current situation) is doubly outlined to call attention to it. It is usually in the lower-right corner of the box. In Figure 3-13, OK is the default button. The user can activate the default button simply by pressing Return or Enter on the keyboard. If there's no default button, Return and Enter have no effect and the user must click in one of the screen buttons.

A special type of modal dialog box is one with no buttons. This type of box just informs the user of a situation without eliciting any response. It usually describes the progress of an ongoing operation, then disappears. Because it has no buttons, the user has no way to control or dismiss it. It must remain on the screen long enough for the user to read it.

A **modeless dialog box** allows the user to perform other operations without dismissing the dialog box. Figure 3-14 shows an example of a modeless dialog box.

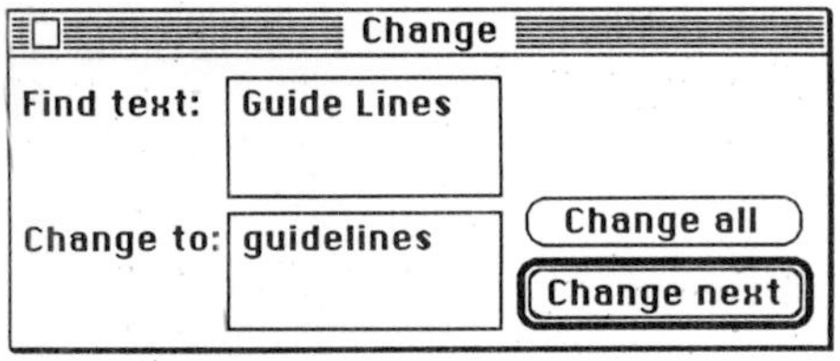

Figure 3-14
A modeless dialog box

A modeless dialog box is dismissed by clicking in the close box or by choosing Close. The dialog box is also dismissed implicitly when the user chooses Quit. The application should remember the contents of the dialog box after the box is dismissed, so that when the application is opened again, the dialog box can be restored exactly as it was.

Controls work the same way in modeless dialog boxes as in modal dialog boxes, except that buttons never dismiss the dialog box. In this context, the OK button means "go ahead and perform the operation, but leave the dialog box up," whereas the Cancel button usually terminates an ongoing operation.

A modeless dialog box can also have text fields, which the user can edit with the commands in the Edit menu.

Alerts

Every user is likely at one time or another to do something that an application can't cope with. Applications occasionally have to call the user's attention to such things as a loose mouse connection or lack of paper in the printer. **Alerts** let applications respond to problems in a consistent way, and in stages according to the severity of the problem, the user's expertise, and the particular history of the problem. The two kinds of alerts are beeps and alert boxes.

Beeps

Beeps are used for errors that are both minor and immediately obvious. For example, if the user tries to backspace past the left boundary of a text field, the application can simply beep instead of displaying an alert box. So that people who can't hear don't miss the message, all beeps should be accompanied by a flash (rapid inverting) of the menu bar.

Alert boxes

An alert box resembles a modal dialog box (see Figure 3-13). The only way the user can respond is by clicking buttons or by pressing Enter or Return. Alert boxes might contain dials and buttons but usually not text fields, radio buttons, or check boxes.

Note the recommended general arrangement of the elements. The icon is at the left, with the message text to the right. The buttons are below the message, with the default button, boldly outlined, at the lower right. The default is the likeliest or safest response, and can be chosen by simply pressing Return or Enter.

The way to be sure the default button is really "safe" is to word the message carefully. Messages in alert boxes must be brief, informative, and friendly without being misleading. If the alert is warning the user of a serious situation, it must be made clear—not hidden in a polite phrase. Messages should be phrased so that the user can easily answer them, and the wording should reflect the user's point of view, not the programmer's. Figure 3-15 shows an example.

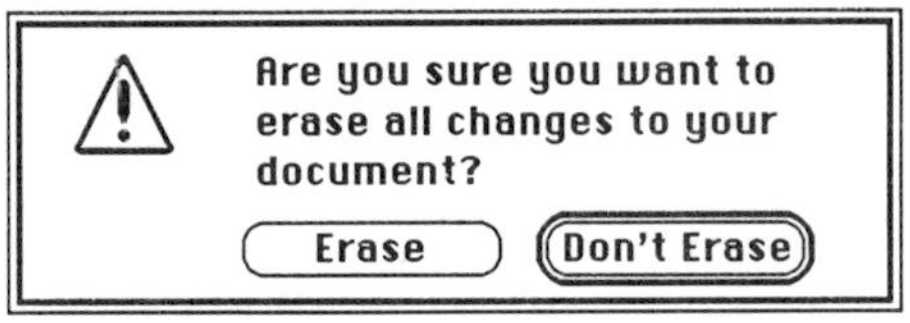

Figure 3-15
A typical alert box

There are three classes of alert boxes, each for a different kind of situation and each having its own icon (Figure 3-16).

- **Note.** Provides information about situations that have no drastic effects. The user usually responds by pressing an OK button.

- **Caution.** Calls attention to an operation that may have undesirable results if it's allowed to continue. The user is given the choice to continue or not.

- **Stop.** Calls attention to a serious problem that requires the user to choose from alternative courses of action.

Note   Caution   Stop

Figure 3-16
Alert box icons

An application can define different responses for each of several stages of an alert, so that if the user persists in the same mistake, the application can issue increasingly helpful (or increasingly stern) messages. A typical sequence is for the first two consecutive occurrences of the mistake to result in a beep, and for subsequent occurrences to result in an alert box. This type of sequence is especially appropriate when the mistake is likely to be accidental (for example, when the user chooses Cut when there's no text selection).

How the buttons in an alert box are labeled depends on the nature of the box. If the box presents the user with a situation in which no alternative actions are available, the box has a single button that's labeled OK. Clicking this button means "I've read the alert." If the user is given alternatives, then typically the alert is phrased as a question that can be answered Yes or No. In this case, buttons labeled Yes and No are appropriate, although variations such as Save and Don't Save are also acceptable. OK and Cancel can be used, as long as their meanings aren't ambiguous.

Generally, it's better to be polite than abrupt, even if it means lengthening the message. The role of the alert box is to be helpful and make constructive suggestions, not to give orders. But its focus is to help the user solve the problem, not to give an academic (no matter how interesting) description of the problem itself. It's important to phrase messages in alert boxes so that users aren't left guessing the real meaning.

Make alert messages self-explanatory. The user should never have to refer to a manual or reference card to find out what an alert message means. Test your alert messages to be sure they tell the user exactly what needs to be done.

The best way to make an alert message understandable is to think carefully through the error condition itself. Can the application handle this without an error? Is the error specific enough so that the user can fix the situation? What are the recommended solutions? Can the exact item causing the error be displayed in the alert message?

Desk accessories

A desk accessory is a program with a relatively limited scope that can be opened while another application is running. Desk accessories can be created to perform a wide range of functions. Some imitate useful objects found on real desktops—the standard Macintosh Note Pad, Alarm Clock, and Calculator, for example. Some (the Chooser, for example) are file- or network-related utilities that users may need to access from within a number of different applications. Some are specific to an application or type of application, such as rulers and other graphics tools that are available only in graphics applications, and spelling checkers that are needed only when a word processing application is being used. There are also "idle" programs that blank out the screen or display special graphics after the computer has been idle for a specified period of time. Figure 3-17 shows some desk accessories on a desktop.

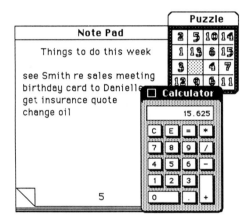

Figure 3-17
Some desk accessories

The user can quickly open one or more desk accessories by choosing them from the Apple menu. Generally, all installed desk accessories can be accessed from the Finder or from any other application, except for desk accessories specific to a particular application or type of application.

Don't design a full-scale application and implement it as a desk accessory. If it's really an application, treat it as an application. Remember that there is a limit on the number of desk accessories that can be installed at one time. On the other hand, if your application is a relatively small one that is useful in a variety of situations, consider making it a desk accessory.

Desk accessories don't have to be windows, but desk accessories that are windows should behave like windows. The user should be able to move them around the screen and dismiss them by clicking a close box.

A desk accessory can add one (and only one) menu to the application's menu bar. This menu goes away when the desk accessory is closed. Desk accessories should never interfere with the application's menus.

If possible, let users install and remove all desk accessories in one standard way. Users should be able to install all Macintosh desk accessories with the standard Font/DA Mover rather than with a special installation program.

All applications should treat desk accessories in a standard way. If a desk accessory opens a window, that window should remain open on the desktop until the user explicitly closes it or quits the current application. The principle "the user is in control" suggests that an application should not close desk accessories just because the user opens or closes document windows. When help systems are implemented as desk accessories, for example, the user can open and close document windows without losing the help window.

There's more on desk accessories under the heading "The Apple Menu" in this chapter.

Menus

Menus make it possible for the user to browse through and choose among the whole range of available operations. The standard menu structure consists of the menu bar (which displays the menu titles), the menus, and each menu's items (commands).

The menu bar

The menu bar extends across the top of the screen and displays the title of each available menu (Figure 3-18).

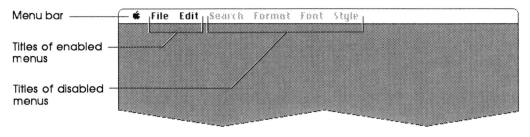

Figure 3-18
Menu bar

If the user moves the pointer to the Edit portion of the menu bar and presses the mouse button, the Edit menu appears, as shown in Figure 3-19. A menu becomes visible when the user selects it by pressing its title.

Nothing but menu titles can appear in the menu bar. Menu titles should remain constant within a given application. If *all* the operations in a given menu are currently disabled (that is, the user can't choose them), the menu title should be dimmed (drawn in gray) but should remain visible in the menu bar. The user must always be able to pull down the menu and *see* the names of the operations even when none of them can, at the moment, be chosen.

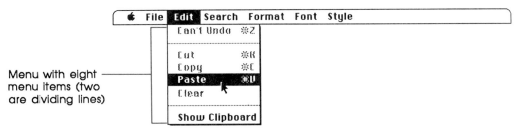

Figure 3-19
Menu

Menu items

Menu items should be either verbs or adjectives. Use verbs (or verb phrases) to show the user what can be *done*—Copy, Find, and Show Page, for example. Use adjectives (or adjective phrases) to let the user specify an attribute of a selected object—Chicago [font], Underline, and Double Space, for example. Adjectives in menus *imply* actions—think of "Chicago" as shorthand for "*change* the selected text to Chicago font." Menu items usually apply to the current selection, although some may apply to the whole document or window.

When you're designing an application program, don't assume that *everything* has to be done through menus. Menus are often the best method, but sometimes it's more appropriate for an operation to take place as a result of direct user manipulation of a graphic object on the screen, such as a control or icon. Alternatively, a single menu item can start to execute complicated instructions by bringing up a dialog box for the user to fill in.

Choosing a menu item

To choose a menu item, the user positions the pointer over the menu's title in the menu bar, and presses the mouse button. The application highlights the title and displays the menu.

While holding down the mouse button, the user drags the pointer through the menu. Each menu item is highlighted in turn. When the user releases the mouse button, the operation that's highlighted is chosen. As soon as the mouse button is released, the menu item blinks briefly, the menu disappears, and the operation is executed. The menu title in the menu bar remains highlighted until the operation is completed.

Nothing actually happens until the user chooses the operation. The user can *look* at any of the menus without making a commitment to do anything. The user can also move the pointer all over the screen (except back into the menu bar) without losing sight of the menu, as long as the mouse button is pressed. To close a pull-down menu without choosing an operation, the user simply returns the pointer to the menu bar or moves it away from the menu, then releases the button.

Appearance of menu items

The items in a particular menu should be logically related to the title of the menu. Menu items must be terse, preferably one word with the first letter capitalized. If it's necessary to use more than one word (Save As or Page Setup, for example), capitalize all important words in the name. In addition to the names, three features of menus help the user understand what each item does: grouping, toggles, and special visual features.

Grouping operations in menus

The most frequently used operations should be at the top of a menu. The least frequently used (such as Quit) should be at the bottom.

As already mentioned, there are two kinds of menu items: actions (verbs) and attributes (adjectives). An attribute stays in effect until it's canceled, whereas an action ceases to be relevant after it has been performed. A single menu can contain both actions and attributes, but the actions should be grouped together and the attributes grouped together. The groups are separated by dotted lines (the dotted lines are actually disabled menu items that are "named" with a horizontal line; Figure 3-22 illustrates these visual features of menus).

Another reason to group operations is to break up a menu so it's easier to read. Operations grouped for this reason are logically related, but independent. Operations that are actions are usually grouped this way, such as Cut, Copy, Paste, and Clear in the Edit menu.

Attribute operations that are interdependent are grouped, either as mutually exclusive groups or as accumulating groups.

In a **mutually exclusive attribute** group, only one item in the group is in effect at any one time. The item that's in effect is preceded in the menu by a check mark. If the user chooses a different item in the group, the check mark is moved to the new item. An example is the Finder's View menu, in which only one view at a time can be in effect (Figure 3-20). (Radio button controls, in which pressing one button in a group disables all the others, are also examples of mutually exclusive attribute groups.)

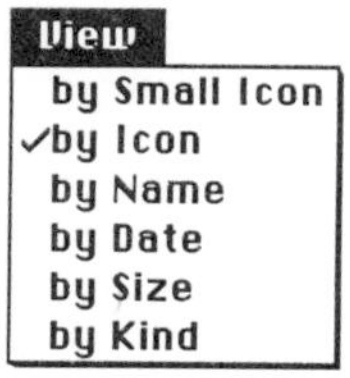

View
by Small Icon
✓by Icon
by Name
by Date
by Size
by Kind

Figure 3-20
View menu

In an **accumulating attribute** group, any number of attributes can be in effect at the same time. One of the items in the group cancels all the others. An example is the standard Style menu, in which the user can choose any combination of Bold, Italic, Underline, Outline, or Shadow—but Plain Text cancels all the others. (Check-box controls, in which all, none, or any other number of the boxes may be in effect at a time, are also examples of accumulating attributes.)

Toggled menu items

Another way to show the presence or absence of an attribute is with a **toggled operation.** A toggled attribute has two states, and a single menu item allows the user to "toggle" between the states. You can show the user that an operation is toggled either with check marks or by changing the wording.

Here's an example of changing the wording in a toggled menu item. When rulers are showing in a program that uses rulers, one item in the Format menu is Hide Rulers. If the user chooses this item, the rulers are hidden, and the name changes to Show Rulers (Figure 3-21). Use this technique only when the wording of the items makes it obvious that they're opposite states of the same attribute—it's better to use verbs (Turn on.../Turn off... or Hide.../Show...) rather than nouns for this sort of menu item. Undo and Redo is another good example.

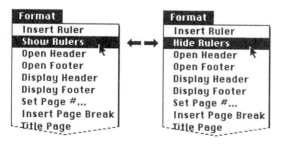

Figure 3-21
Toggled operations

Special visual features

In addition to the way menu items are name and grouped, menus have other features that provide added information:

□ An ellipsis (...) after a menu item means that after the item is chosen, the user will be asked for more information before the operation is carried out. Usually, the user must fill in a dialog box and click an OK button or its equivalent. Don't use the ellipsis when the dialog box that will appear is merely a confirmation or warning (for example, "Save changes before quitting?").

□ Check marks indicate attributes that are currently in effect.

□ Any menu items that the user can't choose at the moment are displayed in gray letters. If the user moves the pointer over a dimmed item, that item isn't highlighted.

□ If an item has a keyboard equivalent (if it can be chosen from the keyboard as well as from a menu), its name in the menu is followed by the Apple (or cloverleaf) symbol and a character. To choose an item this way, the user presses the character key while holding down the Apple (Command) key.

Figure 3-22 illustrates these features.

Several other menu features are also supported:

□ In the Style menu only, menu items can be shown in Bold, Italic, Outline, Underline, or Shadow, to illustrate the text styles themselves.

□ A menu item can be preceded by a special character such as √ or ◆ (to indicate which item is in effect). Icons can also appear in menus, but because of their size they require two menu lines.

□ Applications can have special kinds of menus for special situations. A pull-down menu can even be a palette that can be "torn off" the menu bar and moved around the screen (Figure 3-23). See "Palettes" later in this chapter.

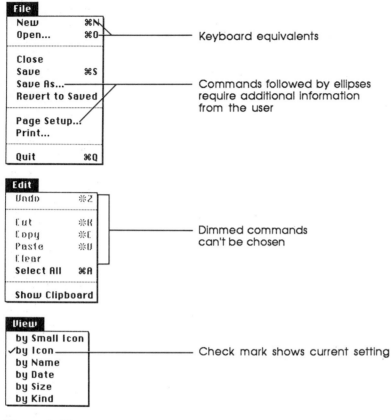

File
New ⌘N
Open... ⌘O
Close
Save ⌘S
Save As...
Revert to Saved
Page Setup...
Print...
Quit ⌘Q
Keyboard equivalents
Commands followed by ellipses require additional information from the user
Edit
Undo
Cut
Copy
Paste
Clear
Select All ⌘A
Show Clipboard
Dimmed commands can't be chosen
View
by Small Icon
✓by Icon
by Name
by Date
by Size
by Kind
Check mark shows current setting

Figure 3-22
Visual features of menus

Fill
None

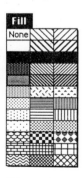

Figure 3-23
A pull-down palette

Scrolling menus

If a menu becomes too long to fit on the screen, an indicator appears at the bottom of the menu to show that there are more items (Figure 3-24). When the user drags over the indicator, the menu scrolls to show the additional items. When the last item is shown, the indicator disappears.

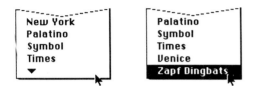

Figure 3-24
Scrolling menu indicator at bottom of menu

As soon as the menu starts scrolling, another indicator appears at the top of the menu to show that some items are now hidden in that direction (Figure 3-25).

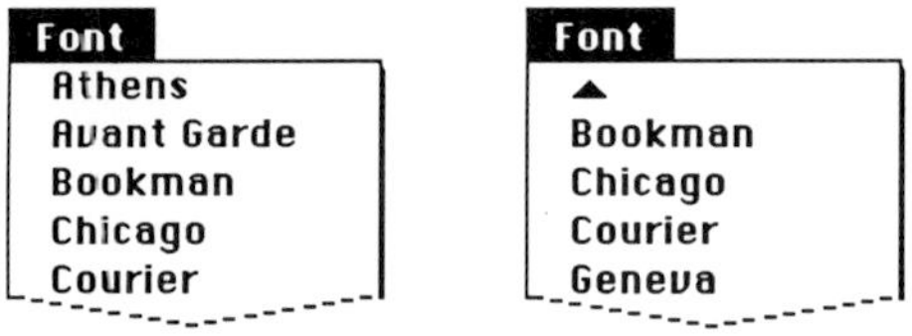

Figure 3-25
Scrolling menu indicator at top of menu

If the user drags back up to the top, the menu scrolls back down in the same manner. If the user lets go of the mouse button or selects another menu, and then selects the original menu again, it appears in its original position, with the hidden items and the indicator at the bottom.

Keyboard equivalents for menu items

There are several menu items, particularly in the File and Edit menus, that commonly have keyboard equivalents. Keyboard equivalents are provided for people who prefer to keep their hands on the keyboard instead of using a pointing device to choose operations from menus.

The letter used for a keyboard equivalent should be mnemonic—it should either be the first letter of the command (or of an important word in the command), or it should have some other relevance (X for Cut, for example) so that the user can remember it. Keyboard equivalents are case independent. In other words, both Apple-S and Apple-s mean *Save*. The keyboard equivalents are shown in the menus as capital letters for consistency and aesthetics. The keyboard equivalent for *Help* in the Apple menu is shown as Apple-?, but it doesn't actually require that the Shift key be pressed. Modifier-key combinations other than the ones listed here should also be case independent.

For the sake of consistency, several of the available keyboard equivalents should be used only for the operations listed below and should never be used for any other purpose.

Apple menu

Apple-?	Help

File menu

Apple-N	New
Apple-O	Open
Apple-S	Save
Apple-Q	Quit

Edit menu

Apple-Z	Undo
Apple-X	Cut
Apple-C	Copy
Apple-V	Paste

Many desk accessories (which are accessible from *all* applications) use the Clipboard and must be able to depend on the keyboard equivalents for Undo, Cut, Copy, and Paste.

The keyboard equivalent for Quit is important in case there's a mouse malfunction. The user can still leave the application in an orderly way (with a dialog box that accepts the Return key as a Yes response), saving any changes made to documents since the documents were last saved.

Note that the Edit menu's four reserved letter keys are in close proximity to each other and to the Apple key, allowing easy one-hand operation.

The keyboard equivalents in the Style menu are less strictly reserved. Applications that have a Style menu shouldn't use these keyboard equivalents for any other purpose, but applications that have no Style menu may use them for any purpose. Remember that you risk confusing users if a given key combination means different things in different applications.

Style menu

Apple-P	Plain text
Apple-B	Bold
Apple-I	Italic
Apple-U	Underline

Interrupting an operation

One other reserved Apple-key combination is not a keyboard equivalent for a menu item. Apple-period (Apple-.) is used to stop the current operation before it completes. The Escape key, on keyboards that have it, does the same thing.

The standard menus

Three menus, the Apple, File, and Edit menus, appear in almost every application. The Font, FontSize, and Style menus, which affect the appearance of text, appear only in applications in which they're relevant.

The Apple menu

Desk accessories are mini-applications that are always available, via the Apple menu, while the Finder or any other application is in use. The list of installed desk accessories is usually alphabetized (Figure 3-26).

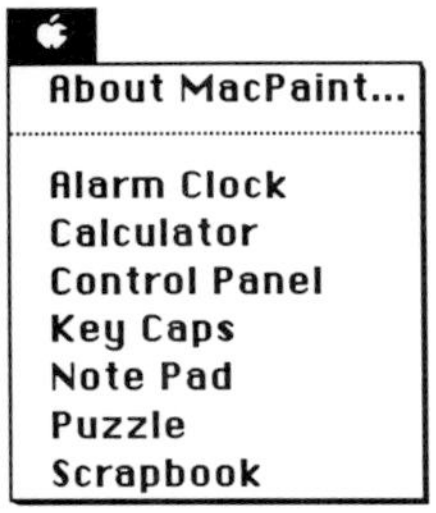

```
 é
┌─────────────────────┐
│ About MacPaint...    │
├ · · · · · · · · · · ·┤
│ Alarm Clock          │
│ Calculator           │
│ Control Panel        │
│ Key Caps             │
│ Note Pad             │
│ Puzzle               │
│ Scrapbook            │
└─────────────────────┘
```

Figure 3-26
The Apple menu

Only those desk accessories installed in the current System file can appear in the Apple menu. There are some desk accessories that are linked to a particular application—for example, spelling checkers that appear in the Apple menu only when a word processing application is active. The list of desk accessories is expanded or reduced according to what's available. There can be more than one accessory on the desktop at one time, as shown in Figure 3-27.

Figure 3-27
Some desk accessories

The Apple menu also contains the About... menu item. Choosing this item brings up a dialog box with the name, version number, and copyright information for the current application, as well as any other information the application developer wants to display. The Help item is also commonly in the Apple menu. In some applications, the Help and About... functions are combined in one menu item.

The File menu

The File menu lets the user perform certain simple filing operations without leaving the application and returning to the Finder (Figure 3-28). It also contains Print and Quit. All of these operations are described below.

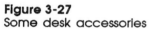

Figure 3-28
Standard File menu

New

Opens a new, untitled document for the current application. The user names the document the first time it's saved. New is disabled when the maximum number of documents allowed by the application is already open.

Open

Opens an existing document. A dialog box lets the user select *which* document. This dialog box shows a list of all the documents on the disk whose name is displayed that can be handled by the current application (Figure 3-29 and Figure 3-30). Which dialog box appears depends on the file system on the disk. With the Macintosh File System (MFS), used on 400K disks, all the documents are displayed together in one list; folders are ignored.

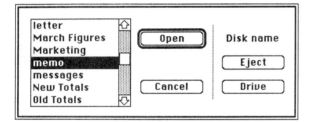

Figure 3-29
MFS Open dialog box

With the Hierarchical File System (HFS) on the Macintosh, the user, when opening a document, can browse through all levels of folders, forward and backward. The Eject and Drive buttons allow the user to look at documents on another disk or to eject a disk. When no disk is available to look at or to eject, these buttons are dimmed.

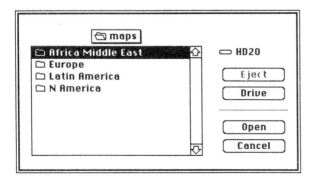

Figure 3-30
HFS Open dialog box

Using Open from an application, the user can open only a document that can be processed by that application. To open a document that can be processed only by some other application, the user must ordinarily leave the application and return to the Finder. Using Open from the Finder, the user can open any document—the appropriate application is automatically opened as well.

When an application starts up by putting an empty untitled document on the screen, the Open option can remain enabled (not dimmed) even if the application allows only one open document at a time. In this case, choosing Open from the File menu simultaneously closes the empty document (why save an empty document?) and opens another.

Close

Closes the active window, which may be a document window, a desk accessory, or any other type of window. Clicking in a window's close box is the same as choosing Close.

When the user chooses Close, and *the active document has been changed* since the last save, the Close dialog box appears, asking "Save changes before closing?" A great deal of work can be lost if a user mistakenly clicks No instead of Yes. To avoid confusion, all applications should use the same standard Close dialog box (Figure 3-31). This is especially important to users who often move from one application to another and become less aware of subtle differences between applications.

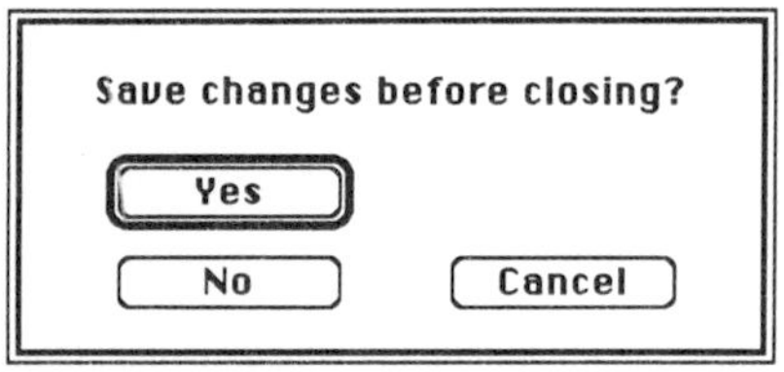

Figure 3-31
Standard Close dialog box

Yes and No, the two direct responses to the question, are placed together on the left side of the box. Yes is the default button. Cancel, which cancels Close, is to the right, separate from Yes and No.

The text of the question is generally "Save changes before closing?" but if the user sees this message after choosing Quit, the text would instead be "Save changes before quitting?" If the application supports multiple windows, the text is "Save changes to [document name] before closing?" Regardless of the text of the question, the box should always look the same and appear in the same place on the screen.

Save

Lets the user save the active document to a disk, including any changes made to that document since the last time it was saved. The document remains open. Users appreciate seeing, at this point, a message telling them the document is indeed being saved.

If the user chooses Save for a new untitled document (one the user hasn't named yet), the application presents the Save As dialog box (described next). This dialog box allows the user to name the document and choose where it will be saved before the application continues with the save. The active document remains active.

If there's not enough room on the disk to save the document, the application says so. The application then suggests that the user can choose Save As instead, to save the document on another disk.

Save As

Saves a copy of the active document under a new name provided by the user. When the user opens a document, makes changes to it, and then chooses Save As, the changes are not made to the original document. The changed version of the document is saved under the new name. The active document is no longer the one the user opened, but rather the new one with the new name.

If no changes had been made to the original document when Save As was chosen, then there are two identical documents having different names.

In applications that support stationery, the Save As dialog box includes a Stationery option. A document that is saved as stationery becomes a template containing whatever information was in the original document. Figure 3-32 shows a Save As dialog box with a Stationery option.

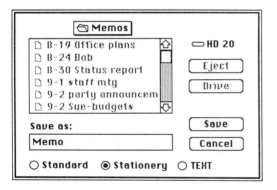

Figure 3-32
A Save As dialog box

If stationery called "Memo" is opened, a document with the default name "Memo #1" is opened (then "Memo #2" and so on). When this document is saved, the Save As dialog box appears again, so that the user can rename the document if desired.

Revert to Saved

Discards all changes made to the active document since the last time it was saved or opened. The document on disk is reopened. Before all this happens, a dialog box lets the user confirm that this is what he or she really wants. (This follows the principles that users should be allowed to make informed decisions and to change their minds.) Figure 3-33 shows a Revert to Saved dialog box.

```
  /!\    Revert to the last version
         saved?

Caution  [  Cancel  ]  [|    OK    |]
```

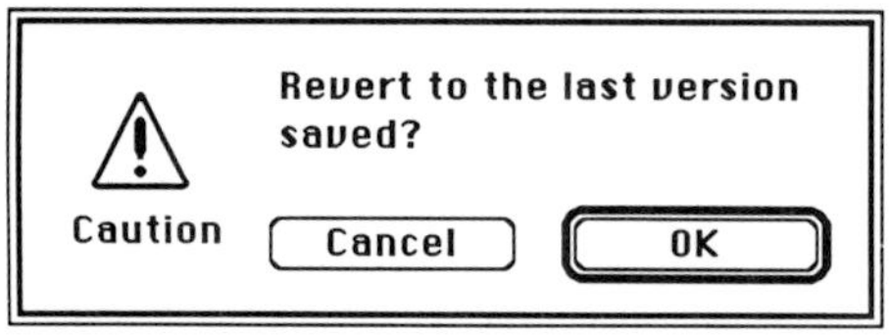

Figure 3-33
A Revert to Saved dialog box

Page Setup

Lets the user specify printing parameters such as the paper size and printing orientation (different applications will provide different options as needed). These parameters are saved with the document when the document is saved. Figure 3-34 shows a Page Setup dialog box.

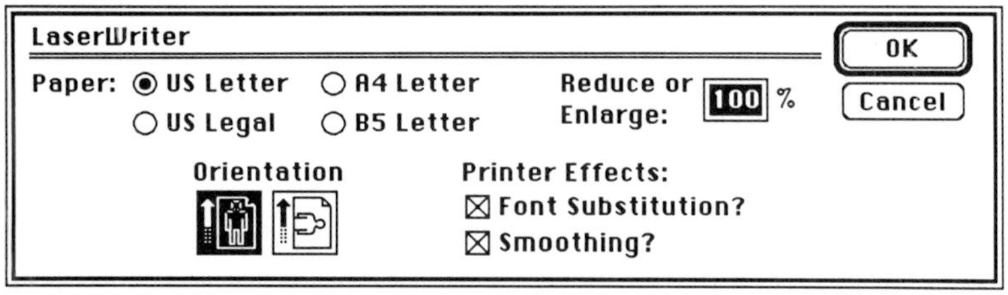

```
LaserWriter                                    [    OK    ]
Paper:  ⦿ US Letter  ○ A4 Letter   Reduce or [100] %
        ○ US Legal   ○ B5 Letter   Enlarge:        [  Cancel  ]

           Orientation         Printer Effects:
           [🯅][🯅]             ⊠ Font Substitution?
                               ⊠ Smoothing?
```

Figure 3-34
A Page Setup dialog box

Print

Lets the user specify various parameters, such as print quality and number of copies, and then prints the document. The parameters apply only to the current printing operation and are not saved with the document. Figure 3-35 shows a Print dialog box.

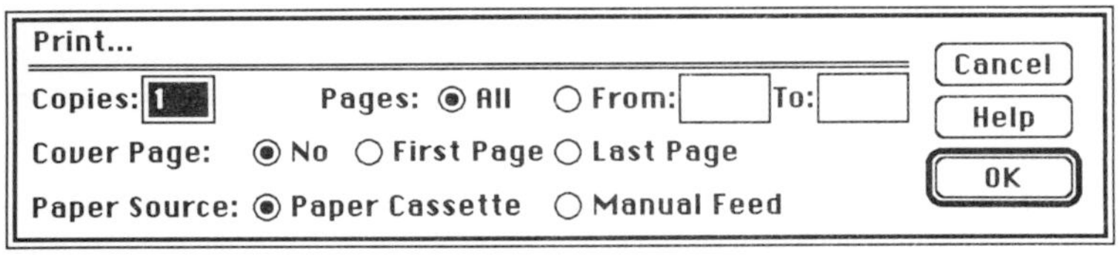

```
┌──────────────────────────────────────────────────────────┐
│ Print...                                                   │
│                                          ┌──────────┐      │
│ Copies:│1 │   Pages: ⦿ All  ○ From:│  │To:│  │ │ Cancel  │ │
│                                          └──────────┘      │
│ Cover Page:  ⦿ No  ○ First Page ○ Last Page  │  Help  │   │
│                                          ┌──────────┐      │
│ Paper Source: ⦿ Paper Cassette  ○ Manual Feed │  OK  │    │
│                                          └──────────┘      │
└──────────────────────────────────────────────────────────┘
```

Figure 3-35
A Print dialog box

Quit

Lets the user leave the application and return to the Finder. If any open documents have been changed since the last time they were saved, the application presents the "Save changes?" dialog box, once for each open document.

The Edit menu

There are two important principles behind the Edit menu:

☐ Anything the user can do, the user can also undo.

☐ Data can easily be moved from one part of a document to another part, from one document to another, and even between documents that are created by different applications or desk accessories. The Clipboard, a holding area for text or graphics, makes this possible.

The Edit menu allows access to the operations that cut, copy, and paste selections, as well as to Undo, Select All, and Show Clipboard. You can add other items to the Edit menu if your application requires them—and if they're related to the standard items already there.

All applications should support Undo, Cut, and Paste. This requires that the first five lines in the Edit menu be exactly as shown in Figure 3-36: Undo followed by a dotted line, then Cut, Copy, Paste, and Clear. Consistency in this menu is important even if your application doesn't itself make use of Undo, Cut, and Paste—these features are available to desk accessories only through the Edit menu.

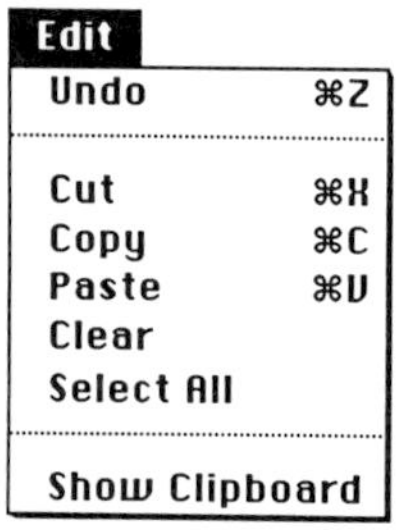

```
┌─────────────────────────┐
│ ■Edit■                  │
│ Undo          ⌘Z        │
│·························  │
│ Cut           ⌘H        │
│ Copy          ⌘C        │
│ Paste         ⌘U        │
│ Clear                   │
│ Select All              │
│·························  │
│ Show Clipboard          │
└─────────────────────────┘
```

Figure 3-36
Standard Edit menu

The Clipboard

The Clipboard holds whatever is cut or copied from a document. Its contents stay intact when the user changes documents, opens a desk accessory, or leaves the application. An application can show the contents of the Clipboard in a window and can choose whether to have the Clipboard window open or closed when the application starts up.

The Clipboard window looks like a document window. The user can see its contents but cannot edit them. In other respects, the Clipboard window behaves like any other window.

Every time the user performs a Copy on the current selection, a copy of the selection replaces the previous contents of the Clipboard. The previous contents of the Clipboard remain available in case the user chooses Undo.

The Clipboard is available to all applications that support Cut, Copy, and Paste. The user can see the Clipboard window by choosing Show Clipboard from the Edit menu. If the Clipboard window is already showing, the user can hide it by clicking the close box or choosing Hide Clipboard from the Edit menu. (Show Clipboard and Hide Clipboard are a single toggled item.)

Because the content of the Clipboard doesn't change when the user moves from one application to another, or when the user opens a desk accessory, the Clipboard is used for transferring data among compatible applications and desk accessories.

If the Clipboard file is moved from one disk to another, the contents move with it, replacing any existing Clipboard file on the target disk.

Undo

The Undo menu item reverses the effect of the previous operation. Not all operations can be undone. The application determines *which* operations can be undone. The general rule is that operations that change the contents of the document can be undone, whereas operations that don't change the contents of the document cannot be undone.

Most menu items (whether chosen from the menu or by a keyboard equivalent) can be undone. A typing sequence (any sequence of characters typed from the keyboard or numeric keypad, including Backspace, Return, and Tab, but *not* including keyboard equivalents of menu items) can also be undone.

Operations that can't be undone include selecting, scrolling, and splitting the window or changing a window's size or location. None of these operations interrupts a typing sequence. For example, if the user types a few characters and then scrolls the document, an Undo operation doesn't undo the scrolling but *does* undo the typing. Whenever the location affected by the Undo operation isn't currently showing on the screen, the application should scroll the document so the user can see the effect of the Undo.

The actual wording of the Undo line, as it appears in the Edit menu, is Undo Typing or Undo Cut—whatever the last undoable operation was. If the last operation can't be undone, the line reads simply Undo and is dimmed to indicate that it's disabled.

Figure 3-37 illustrates Undo and Redo in an Edit menu.

Edit			**Edit**	
Undo Typing ⌘Z	⬅ ➡		**Redo Typing ⌘Z**	
Cut	⌘H		Cut	⌘H
Copy	⌘C		Copy	⌘C
Paste	⌘U		Paste	⌘U
Clear			Clear	
Select All			Select All	
Show Clipboard			Show Clipboard	

Figure 3-37
Undo and Redo in an Edit menu

If the last operation was Undo, the menu item is *Redo xxx*, where *xxx* is the operation that was undone. If the user chooses Redo, the Undo is undone.

The Apple-Z key combination is reserved as a keyboard substitute for Undo/Redo in the Edit menu and should be used for no other purpose.

Cut

The user chooses Cut either to delete the current selection or to move it. A move is eventually completed by choosing Paste.

When the user chooses Cut, the application removes the current selection from the document and puts it in the Clipboard, replacing the Clipboard's previous contents. The place where the selection used to be becomes the new selection; the visual implications of this vary among applications. For example, in text, the new selection is an insertion point; in an array, it's an empty but highlighted cell. If the user chooses Paste immediately after choosing Cut, the document is just as it was before the Cut.

The Apple-X key combination is reserved as a keyboard substitute for the Cut operation in the Edit menu and should be used for no other purpose.

Copy

Before copying something, the user must first select it. Copy puts a duplicate of the selection in the Clipboard, but the selection also remains in the document. The user can then move the insertion point and choose Paste to insert the Clipboard's contents somewhere else.

The Apple-C key combination is reserved as a keyboard substitute for Copy in the Edit menu and should be used for no other purpose.

Paste

Paste is the last stage of a move or copy operation. It inserts the contents of the Clipboard into the document, replacing the current selection. If there is no current selection, it's inserted at the insertion point. The user can choose Paste several times in a row to paste multiple copies. After a paste, the new selection is the object that was pasted, except in text, where it's an insertion point immediately after the pasted text. The Clipboard remains unchanged.

The Apple-V key combination is reserved as a keyboard substitute for Paste in the Edit menu and should be used for no other purpose.

Clear

When the user makes a selection and then either chooses Clear from the Edit menu or presses the Backspace key (Delete key on some keyboards) or the Clear key, the application deletes the highlighted selection. Unlike Cut and Copy, the Clear operation does not put the selection in the Clipboard. The Clipboard is unchanged and the new selection is the same as it would be after a cut.

Select All

Select All selects every object in the document. In a word processing application, Select All selects every character as well as all graphics in the document (making it very easy to reformat or copy an entire document).

Show Clipboard

Show Clipboard is a toggled item. When the clipboard isn't displayed, the menu lists Show Clipboard. If the user chooses Show Clipboard, the clipboard window is displayed and the wording in the menu changes to Hide Clipboard.

Font-related menus

Three standard menus affect the appearance of text. The Font menu lets the user determine the font of a text selection or of the characters about to be typed. The FontSize menu lets the user determine the size, in points, of the characters. The Style menu lets the user determine such aspects of the text's appearance as boldface, italic, and so on.

A **font** (also often called a typeface) is a set of typographical characters created with a consistent design. All the characters in a font share such features as the thickness of vertical and horizontal lines, the degree and position of curves, and the use or absence of serifs. Serifs are fine lines added to the main strokes of a letter. The text of this book is set in various sizes and styles of a serif font. The section headings in this book, on the other hand, are set in a sans serif font, which has no serifs. The characters in a font can appear in many different point sizes, but all have the same general appearance, regardless of size. Because fonts can be either fixed-width or proportional, an application can't make assumptions about exactly how many characters will fit in a given area.

Font menu

The Font menu lists the fonts that are currently available. A check mark indicates which font is currently in effect. Figure 3-38 illustrates a font menu with some common Macintosh fonts.

```
 Font
 Athens
 Chicago
 Geneva
 London
 Monaco
✓New York
 Venice
```

Figure 3-38
Font menu with some common Macintosh fonts

FontSize menu

Font sizes are measured in **points**. A point is a typographical unit of measure equivalent to 1/72 inch. The FontSize menu lists the nine standard available sizes. The font size currently in effect is indicated with a check mark (Figure 3-39). Not every font is available in all sizes; the sizes that are available for the selected font are shown outlined in the FontSize menu. A font can be **scaled** to the other sizes, but scaled fonts usually suffer in appearance on the screen and when printed by some kinds of printers.

This sentence is in 10-point type. The chapter title on the first page of this chapter is in 18-point type.

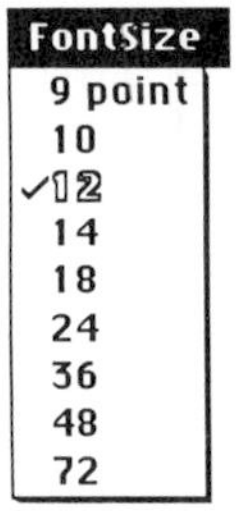

```
 FontSize
 9 point
 10
✓12
 14
 18
 24
 36
 48
 72
```

Figure 3-39
FontSize menu with standard font sizes

If there's insufficient room in the menu bar for the word FontSize, it can be abbreviated to Size. If there's insufficient room for both a Font menu and a Size menu, the sizes can be put at the end of the Style menu.

Style menu

Text-oriented applications, such as word processing programs, have a Style menu (Figure 3-40).

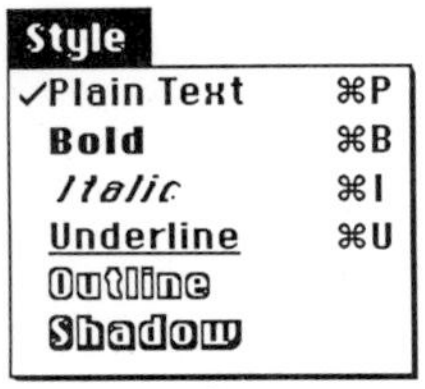

```
┌─────────────────────┐
│ Style               │
├─────────────────────┤
│ ✓Plain Text    ⌘P   │
│ Bold           ⌘B   │
│ Italic         ⌘I   │
│ Underline      ⌘U   │
│ Outline             │
│ Shadow              │
└─────────────────────┘
```

Figure 3-40
Standard Style menu

The operations in the standard Style menu are Plain Text, Bold, Italic, Underline, Outline, and Shadow. Others that can be included here are superscript, subscript, small caps, uppercase, and lowercase. All except Plain Text are accumulating attributes. This means that the user can choose all of them, none of them, or any combination of them. It is important that each attribute can be individually toggled on and off. The user who has accumulated several attributes—bold, italic, and underline, for example—and decides to eliminate bold and italic but keep underline, shouldn't have to choose Plain (which would turn off all three) and then start over by choosing underline.

An attribute that's in effect for the current selection is preceded, in the Style menu, by a check mark. The absence of the check mark indicates that the attribute is not in effect for the current selection. Choosing Plain Text cancels all the other choices.

Other menus use plain 12-point Chicago for their text, but the Style menu can be self-documenting by using, for example, shadowed 12-point Chicago to list the shadowed attribute. Apple-key combinations can be used as keyboard shortcuts to the Style menu.

Special menu types

This section discusses four alternate types of menus: hierarchical menus, pop-up menus, graphic menus called palettes, and a hybrid of palettes and pull-down menus called tear-off menus.

Hierarchical menus

Hierarchical menus are a logical extension of the standard menu metaphor: another dimension is added to a menu, so that a menu item can be the title of a submenu. When the user drags the pointer through a hierarchical menu item, a submenu appears after a brief delay.

Hierarchical menu items have an indicator at the right edge of the menu, as shown in Figure 3-41.

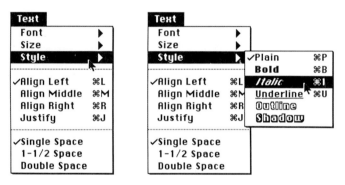

Figure 3-41
Main menu before and after a submenu appears

One main menu can contain both standard menu items and submenus; both levels can have Command-key equivalents. (The submenu title can't have a Command-key equivalent, of course, because it's not a command. Key combinations aren't used to pull down menus.)

Two delay values enable submenus to function smoothly, without jarring distractions to the user. The **submenu delay** is the length of time before a submenu appears as the user drags the pointer through a hierarchical menu item. It prevents flashing caused by rapid appearance-disappearance of submenus. The **drag delay** allows the user to drag diagonally from the submenu title into the submenu, briefly crossing part of the main menu, without the submenu disappearing (which would ordinarily happen when the pointer was dragged into another main menu item). This is illustrated in Figure 3-42.

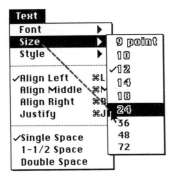

Figure 3-42
Dragging diagonally to a submenu item

Other aspects of submenus—menu blink, and so forth—behave exactly the same way as in standard menus.

Using standard menus, the user can drag the mouse across the menu bar and immediately see *all* of the choices currently available. Although this isn't true when hierarchical menus are used, it's important that this original capability be maintained as much as possible. To keep this essential simplicity and clarity, these guidelines should be followed:

☐ Hierarchical menus are used only for *lists of related items*, such as fonts or font sizes (in this case, the title of the submenu clearly tells what the submenu contains).

☐ *Only one level* of hierarchical menu is used. This one extra layer of menus potentially increases by an order of magnitude the number of menu items that can be used; more layers than this can make an application very confusing.

Pop-up menus

Another type of menu is a pop-up menu. A pop-up menu isn't in the menu bar, but appears somewhere else on the screen (usually in a dialog box) when the user clicks in a particular place.

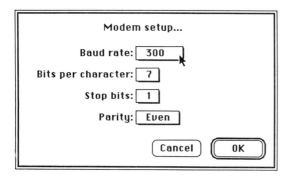

Figure 3-43
A dialog box with pop-up menus

Pop-up menus are used for setting values or choosing from lists of related items. The indication that there is a pop-up menu is a box around the current value, with a one-pixel-thick drop shadow (Figure 3-43). When the user presses on this box, the pop-up menu appears, with the current value—checked and highlighted—under the pointer (Figure 3-44). If the menu has a title, the title highlights while the menu is visible.

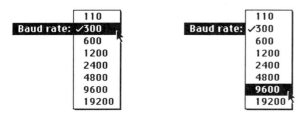

Figure 3-44
A pop-up menu as the pointer is dragged through it

The pop-up menu acts like other menus: the user can move around inside it and choose another item, which then appears highlighted in the box, or can move outside it to leave the current value active. If it reaches the top or bottom of the screen, a pop-up menu scrolls like other menus.

If your application uses pop-up menus, keep the following guidelines in mind:

☐ Pop-up menus are used only for lists of values or related items (similar to hierarchical submenus); they should not be used for commands.

☐ You must draw the shadowed box indicating that there is a pop-up menu, so the user knows that it's there—pop-up menus are never invisible.

☐ While the menu is showing, its title is inverted. If several pop-up menus are near each other, this clears up the possible ambiguity about which one is being chosen from.

□ The current value always appears under the pointer when the menu appears, so that simply clicking on the box doesn't change the item.

□ Don't use hierarchical pop-up menus.

□ Pop-up menus don't have Command-key equivalents.

Always consider whether a pop-up menu is the simplest thing to use in each case, or whether a standard menu or a scrolling box might be more appropriate.

Palettes

Some applications use palettes to provide a quick way for the user to change from one operation to another. A palette is a collection of small symbols, usually enclosed in rectangles. A symbol can be an icon, a pattern, a character, or a drawing that stands for an operation. When the user has clicked on one of the symbols (or in its rectangle), it is distinguished from the other symbols (by highlighting, for example), and the previously highlighted symbol goes back to its normal state. Figure 3-45 shows two palettes from MacPaint.

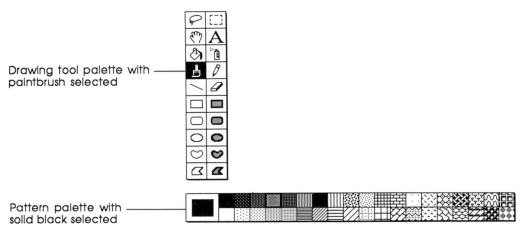

Drawing tool palette with paintbrush selected

Pattern palette with solid black selected

Figure 3-45
Two palettes

Typically, the symbol that's selected determines what operations the user can perform. Selecting a tool from a palette puts the user into a mode. Modes are generally discouraged but can be justified when changing from one mode to another is almost instantaneous and when the user can always see at a glance which mode is in effect. (Changing the shape of the pointer is one way to indicate that a mode has been set.) Like all modal features, palettes should be used only when they're the most natural way to structure an application.

A palette can be either part of a window (as in MacDraw) or separate from the main window (as in MacPaint). Each has its disadvantages. If the palette is part of the window, then parts of the palette may be concealed if the user makes the window smaller. On the other hand, if it's not part of the window, then it takes up extra space on the desktop (in which case it should at least be movable so the user can move it out of the way).

If an application supports multiple open documents but only one palette, the palette reflects the settings for the active window.

Tear-off menus

A tear-off menu is a menu, generally graphic rather than textual, that the user can "tear" from the menu bar and move around the screen like a window. Tear-off menus save desktop space, allow larger windows, and give the user more flexibility than do fixed palettes.

The user can choose a pattern from the tear-off menu shown in Figure 3-46 simply by pulling down the menu like any other menu, then dragging the pointer to the desired pattern and releasing the mouse button.

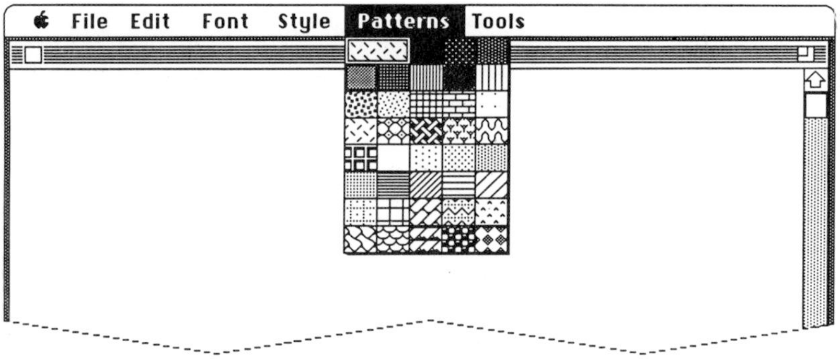

Figure 3-46
Graphic pull-down menu

If the user holds down the Apple key while opening such a menu, then moves the pointer more than ten pixels from any edge of the menu, an outline of the menu follows the pointer. When the mouse button is released, the menu appears at its new location (Figure 3-47).

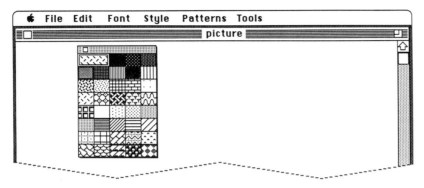

Figure 3-47
Torn-off menu

Even after a menu has been torn off, it can still be accessed from the menu bar. The state of the torn-off menu must be reflected in its pull-down counterpart, and vice versa (Figure 3-48). A given menu can exist in torn-off form only once: if the user tears it off a second time, the first instance disappears.

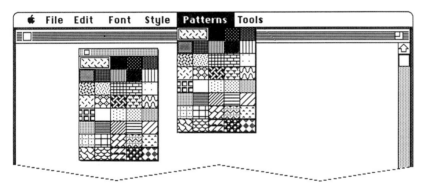

Figure 3-48
Torn-off menu also available in menu bar

Like document windows, torn-off menus can be dragged around the screen and closed with a close box. To avoid confusion, however, tear-off menus don't look exactly like document windows. Tear-off menus are always "in front" of all open document windows. If a single application can have more than one menu torn off at a time, the application must determine their order of precedence.

The pointing device

In most computer systems, the keyboard is the primary input device. In the Apple Desktop Interface, on the other hand, the **pointing device** is central. A pointing device makes possible the direct manipulation that is a central part of the Desktop Interface. The user can communicate with the computer by manipulating graphic objects on the screen. This manipulation is direct because the user can grab (or seem to grab) an object, then indicate what is to be done with it. How do you "grab" an object that you see only as a two-dimensional representation on a glass screen? By pointing at it with a pointing device.

In the Apple Desktop Interface, the standard pointing device is the mouse, but there are other devices (track balls and graphics pens, for example) that perform the same functions. The mouse is a hand-held device, usually (but not necessarily) connected to the computer by a long, flexible cable. There's a single button on the mouse. The user holds the mouse and rolls it on a flat, smooth surface. On the screen, a pointer, which can assume different shapes according to the context of the application, follows the motion of the mouse.

Simply moving the mouse (without pressing the mouse button) just moves the pointer. Most actions take place only when the user positions the pointer over an object on the screen, then presses and releases the mouse button.

Cursors, pointers, and insertion points

Traditional character-oriented command-line interfaces rely on a **cursor** to indicate the place on the display where the next character that is typed will appear. The user uses arrow keys (sometimes called "cursor keys") to move the cursor around the screen. Because there is nothing else to "point" at, no pointer is needed.

In the Desktop Interface, on the other hand, there may be many graphic objects on the screen, unrelated to the text insertion point, to point at. The screen **pointer** is logically attached to the mouse or other pointing device; the user manipulates it to show the application what to do next, and where to do it. What Apple calls an **insertion point** shows where the next characters to be typed will appear. In text, the pointer shows where the insertion point will be moved to if the mouse button is pressed.

Each pointer has a **hot spot**—the portion of the pointer that must be positioned over a screen object before mouse clicks can have an effect on that object. The hot spot should be intuitive, such as the tip of an arrow pointer or the center point of a crosshair pointer. Mouse clicks have an effect only when the pointer's hot spot is positioned over the target object's **hot zone.**

As the pointer moves about the screen, it may change shape. For example, in a text-oriented program the pointer takes the I-beam shape while it's within the text, to show where the insertion point will move to if the mouse button is pressed. When the pointer moves outside the text, it becomes an arrow. Don't confuse the user by changing the pointer's shape without a reason. You might want to have the pointer change shape to give feedback on the range of activities that make sense either in a particular area of the screen or in a current mode. Sometimes, the result of mouse actions depends on the item under the pointer when the mouse button is pressed. Where an application uses modes for different functions, the pointer can be a different shape in each mode. For example, in MacPaint, the pointer shape always reflects the currently selected tool.

Table 3-1 shows some examples of pointers and their effects. You can create additional pointers as needed for other contexts.

Table 3-1
Pointers

Pointer	Name	Used for
▶	Arrow	Scroll bar and other controls, size box, title bar, menu bar, desktop
I	I-beam	Selecting and inserting text
+	Crosshairs	Drawing, shrinking, or stretching graphic objects
⊕	Plus sign	Selecting fields in an array
⌚	Wristwatch	Showing that a lengthy operation is in progress
●	Spinning beachball	Showing that the system is still alive during a lengthy operation

During a particularly lengthy operation, when the user can do nothing but wait until the operation is completed, the pointer may change its shape and become a status or progress indicator. This indicator lets the user know that the system hasn't died— it's just busy. The standard pointer used for this purpose is a wristwatch. Some applications use the "spinning beachball" pointer to show that all is well during longer operations. The kindest applications use a dial to show the passing of time, either in absolute terms or as a proportion of the total, or both. Figure 3-49 is an example.

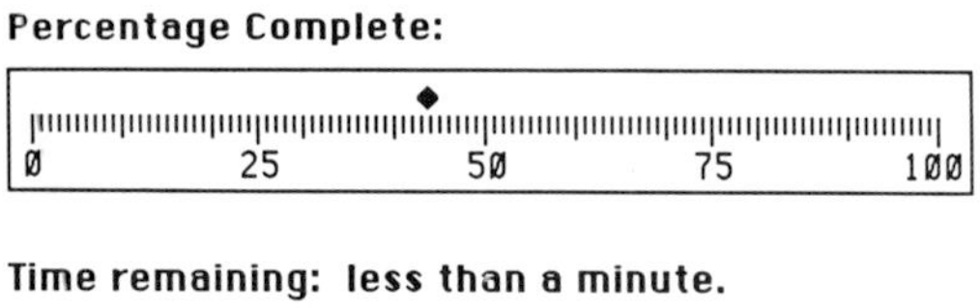

Percentage Complete:

```
         ◆
|||||||||||||||||||||||||||||||||||||||||||||||||||||||||||||||||
0        25        50        75        100
```

Time remaining: less than a minute.

Figure 3-49
The progress dial in AppleLink®

Mouse actions

In general, just *moving* the mouse changes nothing except the location, and possibly the shape, of the pointer. Pressing the mouse button indicates the intention to do something, and releasing the button completes the action. Pressing by itself should have no more effect than clicking has—except in well-defined areas, such as scroll arrows, where it has the same effect as repeated clicking.

The central mouse function is pointing. Other important mouse actions are clicking, double-clicking, pressing, and dragging.

Clicking

Clicking has two components: pushing down on the mouse button and then quickly releasing it while the mouse remains stationary. (If the mouse moves between button down and button up, dragging—not just clicking—is what happens.) Some uses of clicking are to select an object, to move an insertion point, and to turn on a control. The effect of clicking should be immediate and evident. If the function of the click is to cause an action (as when clicking on a button), the *selection is made* when the button is pressed, and the *action takes place* when the button is released.

Double-clicking

Double-clicking involves a second click that follows immediately after the end of a first click. If the two clicks are close enough to one another in terms of time (as set by the user in the Control Panel) and of screen location, then they constitute a double click.

The most common use of double-clicking is as a shortcut way to perform an action. For example, clicking twice on an icon is a faster way to open it than clicking once to select it, then choosing Open from the File menu; clicking twice on a word to select it is faster than dragging through it. Double-clicking can also be used to select a larger object than one that can be selected by a single click.

Double-clicking is a shortcut for those users physically able to use it. Double-clicking must never be the *only* way to perform a given action. Many novice users, children, and disabled people have a hard time double-clicking.

Some applications support selection by double-clicking and triple-clicking. As always with multiple clicks, the second click extends the effect of the first click, and the third click extends the effect of the second click. For example, in a text-oriented application, the first click sets an insertion point, the second click selects the whole word containing the insertion point, and the third click might select the whole sentence or paragraph. In a graphics application, the first click might select a single object, and double and triple clicks might select successively larger sets of objects.

Three clicks is probably the practical limit, and even that is difficult for many people. If an application defines the effect only of single-and double-clicking, a third click should have no effect. If triple-clicking is defined, then the fourth click should have no effect.

Pressing

Pressing means holding the mouse button down for a time while the mouse remains stationary. Pressing on the scroll bar's arrows, for example, causes scrolling until the user releases the mouse button. For certain kinds of objects, pressing on the object has the same effect as clicking it repeatedly. For example, *clicking* a scroll arrow causes a document to scroll one line; *pressing* on a scroll arrow causes the document to scroll continuously until the user releases the mouse button or reaches the end of the document.

Dragging

Dragging means pressing the mouse button, moving the mouse to a new position, and finally releasing the mouse button (Figure 3-50). Dragging can have different effects, depending on what's under the pointer when the mouse button is pressed. The uses of dragging include selecting blocks of text, choosing a menu item, selecting a range of objects, moving an icon or other object from one place to another, and shrinking or expanding an object.

Graphic objects can be moved by dragging. The application either moves the entire object, or attaches a dotted outline of the object to the pointer and moves the outline as the user moves the pointer. When the user releases the mouse button, the application redraws the complete object at the new location.

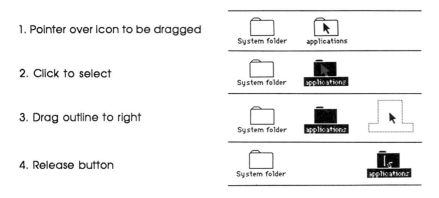

1. Pointer over icon to be dragged

2. Click to select

3. Drag outline to right

4. Release button

Figure 3-50
Dragging with the mouse

An object being moved can be restricted to certain boundaries, such as the edges of a window. If the user moves the pointer outside the boundaries, the application stops drawing the dotted outline of the object. If the user releases the mouse button while the pointer is outside the boundaries, the object doesn't move. If, on the other hand, the user moves the pointer back within the boundaries before releasing the mouse button, the outline is redrawn in the new location. Moving an object beyond the boundary of the window can also cause the window to scroll (autoscroll) or even move the object from one window into another.

Mouse-ahead

Mouse-ahead (analogous to the keyboard's type-ahead) saves, in a memory buffer, any mouse actions the user performs when the application isn't ready to process them. If appropriate, the application can then carry out these stored processes when it has time. Alternatively, the application can choose to ignore saved-up mouse actions, but should do so only to protect the user from possibly damaging consequences.

The keyboard

Because—in the Apple Desktop Interface—the pointing device is used for pointing and manipulating, users don't have to use the keyboard to type commands. The keyboard is used primarily for entering text.

The standard keys on the keyboard are arranged in familiar typewriter fashion. Because keyboards vary from one computer to another, no specific keyboard is illustrated here.

There are two kinds of keys: character keys and modifier keys. A **character key** sends characters to the computer. When held down, a **modifier key** can alter the meaning of the character key being pressed, or alter or amplify the meaning of a mouse action.

Character keys

Character keys include keys for letters, numbers, and punctuation, as well as the Space bar. If the user presses one of these keys while entering text, the corresponding character is added to the text. The Enter, Tab, Return, Backspace (or Delete), Clear, and Escape keys are also treated like character keys. Although the result of pressing one of these keys depends on the application and the context, it is essential that they be used consistently, as described in the following paragraphs.

Enter

The Enter key tells the application that the user is through entering information in a particular area of the document, such as a field in an array. Most applications add information to a document as soon as the user types or draws it. However, the application may need to wait until a whole collection of information is available before processing it. In this case, the user presses the Enter key to signal that the information is complete. Enter (like Return) can be used to dismiss dialog and alert boxes. While the user is entering text into a *text* document, pressing Enter has no effect.

Tab

In text-oriented applications, the Tab key is used to move the insertion point to the next tab stop. In other contexts, Tab is a signal to proceed: it signals movement to the next item in a sequence. Pressing Tab often causes an Enter operation before the tab takes place. While the user is entering text into a *text* document, pressing Tab moves the insertion point to the next tab stop.

Return

The Return key is another signal to proceed, but it defines a different type of motion than Tab. Pressing Return signals movement to the leftmost field one step lower on the display (like a carriage return on a typewriter). Return (like Tab) can cause an Enter operation before the Return operation. Return (like Enter) can be used to dismiss dialog and alert boxes. While the user is entering text into a *text* document, pressing Return moves the insertion point to the beginning of the next line.

Backspace (or Delete)

The Backspace (or Delete) key deletes text or graphics. Generally, if a selection has been made, pressing Backspace (or Delete) deletes the selection without putting it in the Clipboard—and without deleting the character to the left of the insertion point. If there is no selection, pressing Backspace (or Delete) deletes the character to the left of the insertion point without putting it in the Clipboard. The Backspace (or Delete) key has an effect like that of the Clear command in the Edit menu.

Clear

The Clear key has the same effect as the Clear command in the Edit menu; that is, it removes the selection from the document without putting it in the Clipboard. Because not all Apple computers have Clear keys, no application should ever *require* use of the Clear key.

Escape

The Escape key has the general meaning "let me out of here." It's a sort of panic button for the new user. In certain contexts its meaning is specific:

☐ The user can press Escape as a quick way to indicate Cancel in a dialog box.

☐ The user can press Escape to stop an operation in progress, such as printing. (Using Escape this way is like pressing Apple- or Command-period.)

If an application absolutely requires a series of dialog boxes (a fresh look at program design usually eliminates such sequences), the user should be able to use Escape to move backward through the boxes.

Pressing Escape should never cause the user to back out of an operation that would require extensive time or work to reenter. And pressing Escape should never cause the user to lose valuable information. When the user presses Escape during a lengthy operation, the application should display a confirmation dialog box to be sure Escape wasn't pressed accidentally.

Modifier keys

Modifier keys are those that alter the way other keystrokes are interpreted. These keys sometimes affect the way the mouse button is interpreted as well. They are the Shift, Caps Lock, Option, Control, and Apple (or Command) keys. Not all Apple keyboards contain all of these keys. It is important that you use these keys consistently from program to program, as outlined in these guidelines.

Shift

The Shift key, when used together with another character key, produces the uppercase letter on alphabetic keys, or the upper character on two-character keys. The Shift key is also used in conjunction with the mouse for extending a selection (see "Selecting" in this chapter) or for constraining movement in graphics applications—for example, in MacPaint, holding down the Shift key while using the rectangle tool limits the tool to drawing squares.

Caps Lock

The Caps Lock key latches in the down position when pressed, and releases when pressed again. When down it gives the uppercase letter on alphabetic keys. Caps Lock has the same effect on alphabetic keys that the Shift key has, but Caps Lock has *no* effect on any other keys. In other words, even when Caps Lock is down, the user must press the Shift key to produce the uppercase characters (#, ?, and so on) on the nonalphabetic keys.

Option

The Option key, when used together with other keys, produces a set of international characters and special symbols. For example, in many Macintosh fonts, Option-4 produces the ¢ symbol, Option-r produces ®, and Option-g produces ©. Shift and Option can be used together, in combination with a character key, to produce yet other symbols—for example, Option-Shift-? to produce the Spanish ¿ character. The Key Caps desk accessory lets the user preview these combinations in all available fonts. The Option key can also be used in conjunction with the mouse to modify the effect of a click or drag.

The Apple (or Command) key

The Apple key is labeled on different computers with an Apple symbol, a cloverleaf symbol, or both. It has also been known as the Command key or Open Apple key. Pressing a character key while holding down the Apple key usually tells the application to interpret the key as a command, not as a character. In some applications, the Apple key is used with other keys to provide special functions or shortcuts—for example, pressing Apple-Shift-3 on a Macintosh saves, on disk, a snapshot of the current screen. The Apple (or Command) key can also be used in conjunction with the mouse to modify the effect of a click or drag.

The Control key

The Control key is used with terminal-emulation programs for control-key sequences. For all other applications, it is reserved for end-user–defined shortcut key sequences using a macro-key facility.

Type-ahead and auto-repeat

If the user types when the computer is unable to process the keystrokes immediately, or types more quickly than the computer can handle, the extra keystrokes are queued for later processing. This queuing is called **type-ahead.** There's a limit (varying with the computer) to the number of keystrokes that can be queued, but the limit is usually not reached unless the user types while the application is performing a lengthy operation.

When a character key is held down for a certain amount of time, it starts repeating automatically. This feature is called **auto-repeat.** The user can set the delay and the rate of repetition with the Control Panel desk accessory. An application can tell whether a series of keystrokes was generated by auto-repeat or by pressing the same key several times. It can choose to disregard keystrokes generated by auto-repeat; this is usually a good idea for menu commands chosen with Apple-key combinations.

Holding down a modifier key has the same effect as pressing it once. However, if the user holds down a modifier key and a character key at the same time, the effect is the same as if the user held down the modifier key while pressing the character key repeatedly.

Auto-repeat does not function during type-ahead. It operates only when the application is ready to accept keyboard input.

International keyboards

Keyboards used in the United States resemble those on standard American office typewriters. The layout of the international version is designed to conform to the International Standards Organization (ISO) standard. In different countries, international keyboards have different labels on the keys, but the overall *layout* is the same.

Arrow keys

Some Apple keyboards include four arrow keys: Up Arrow, Down Arrow, Left Arrow, and Right Arrow (Figure 3-51).

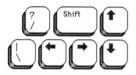

Figure 3-51
Macintosh Plus arrow keys

Appropriate uses for the arrow keys

As a general rule, arrow keys are used to move the insertion point and (when used in tandem with the Shift key) to expand or shrink selections. These guidelines apply both to moving the insertion point and to making selections. In a graphics application, the arrow keys can be used for fine movement (one pixel per keystroke) of selected objects, after the mouse has been used for larger movements. *Arrow keys are never used to duplicate the function of the scroll bars or to move the mouse pointer.*

The arrow keys *do not replace the pointing device.* They can be used as a shortcut way to move the insertion point, and, under some circumstances, to make selections. The guidelines in this section are the minimum guidelines for arrow keys; you can expand on them if you need to, keeping in mind the spirit of these guidelines.

An application should use the arrow keys only when appropriate to the task. Applications that deal with text or arrays (word processors, spreadsheets, and data bases, for example) have an insertion point. This insertion point could be moved both by the mouse and by the arrow keys.

Graphics applications have no insertion point. If a graphics application uses arrow keys, it should be only to move the selected object by the smallest possible increment (one pixel or one grid unit). Graphics applications should never use arrow keys to change a selection or use modifier keys to multiply the effect of arrow keys.

Moving the insertion point

The Left Arrow and Right Arrow keys move the insertion point one character left and right, respectively. Up Arrow and Down Arrow move the insertion point up and down one line, respectively.

During vertical movement of the insertion point, horizontal screen position is maintained in terms of screen pixels, not characters. (Character boundaries seldom line up vertically when proportional fonts are used.) When the insertion point moves to a new line, move it slightly left or right, to the nearest character boundary on the new line. During successive movements up or down, the application should keep the insertion point as close as possible to the original horizontal position as it moves from line to line.

Moving the insertion point in empty documents

Various text-editing programs treat empty documents in different ways. Some assume that an empty document contains no characters, in which case clicking at the bottom of a blank screen causes the insertion point to appear at the top. In this situation, Down Arrow cannot move the insertion point into the blank space (because there are no characters there).

Other applications treat an empty document as a page of space characters, in which case clicking at the bottom of a blank screen puts the insertion point where the user clicked and lets the user type characters there, overwriting the spaces. In this sort of application, Down Arrow moves the insertion point straight down through the spaces.

Whichever of these methods you choose for your application, it's essential that you be consistent throughout.

Using modifier keys with arrow keys

Holding down the Apple key while pressing an arrow key should move the insertion point to the appropriate edge of the window. If the insertion point is already at the edge of the window, then the document is scrolled one windowful in the appropriate direction and the insertion point moves to the same edge of the new windowful. Apple-Up Arrow moves the insertion point to the top of the window, Apple-Down Arrow to the bottom, Apple-Left Arrow to the left edge, and Apple-Right Arrow to the right edge.

With respect to the arrow keys, the Option key is reserved as a "semantic modifier." The application determines what the semantic units are. For example, in a word processor, where the basic semantic unit is the word, Option-Left Arrow and Option-Right Arrow might move the insertion point to the beginning and end, respectively, of a word. (Movement of the insertion point by word boundaries should use the same definition of *word* that the application uses for double-clicking.) In a programming-language editor, where the basic semantic unit is the token, Option- Left Arrow and Option-Right Arrow might move the insertion point left and right to the beginning and end of the token, respectively.

In an application (such as a spreadsheet) that represents itself as an array, the basic semantic unit would be the cell. Option-Left Arrow would designate the cell to the left of the currently active cell as the new active cell, and so on. Using modifier keys with arrow keys doesn't do anything to the data; Option-Left Arrow just performs an Enter and moves the selection to the next cell to the left.

Though the use of multiple modifier-key combinations (such as Apple-Option-Left Arrow) is discouraged, it's all right to use the Shift key with any *one* of the other modifier keys for making a selection. (See "Making a Selection With Arrow Keys" later in this chapter.) If multiple keys must be pressed simultaneously, they should be fairly close together—otherwise many people won't be able to use that combination.

Function keys

Some Apple keyboards include function keys. There are two types of function keys, dedicated and nondedicated. The nondedicated function keys—labeled F1 through F15—are definable by the user, *not* by the application. F1 through F4 represent Undo, Cut, Copy, and Paste in any applications that use these commands.

The six dedicated function keys are labeled Help, Del, Home, End, Page up, and Page down. These keys are used as follows:

- **Help.** Pressing the Help key should produce help; this is equivalent to pressing Command-? (or Command-/). The sort of help available varies among applications; if a full, contextual help system is not available, some sort of useful help screen should be provided.

- **Del.** Pressing Del performs a forward delete: the character directly to the right of the insertion point is removed, shifting everything to the right of the removed character one character position back. The effect is that the insertion point remains stable while it "vacuums" everything ahead of it.

  If Del is pressed when there is a current selection, it has the same effect as pressing Delete (Backspace) or choosing Clear from the Edit menu.

- **Home.** Pressing the Home key is equivalent to moving the scroll boxes (elevators) all the way to the top of the vertical scroll bar and to the left end of the horizontal scroll bar. *It has no effect on the location of the insertion point or any selected material.*

- **End.** This is the opposite of Home: it's equivalent to moving the scroll boxes (elevators) all the way to the bottom of the vertical scroll bar and to the right end of the horizontal scroll bar. *It has no effect on the location of the insertion point or any selected material.*

- **Page up.** This is equivalent to clicking the mouse pointer in the upper gray region of the vertical scroll bar. *It has no effect on the location of the insertion point or any selected material.*

- **Page down.** This is equivalent to clicking the mouse pointer in the lower gray region of the vertical scroll bar. *It has no effect on the location of the insertion point or any selected material.*

Selecting

Before performing an operation on an object (or several objects), the user must select it, usually by clicking on it, to distinguish it from other objects. Selecting the thing to be operated on before identifying the operation itself is a fundamental characteristic of the Apple human interface. The pattern is usually something like this:

1. The user selects an object (a noun, the thing to be operated on).

2. The user chooses an operation (a verb, the thing to be done).

This is sometimes called the "noun-verb paradigm" or "Hey, you—do this!"

There is always a visual cue to show that something has been selected. For example, text and icons in a monochrome environment usually appear in inverse video when selected. In some situations, other forms of highlighting may be more appropriate. The important thing is that there should always be immediate feedback, so the user knows that the click had an effect.

Selecting an object never alters the object itself. Making a selection shouldn't commit the user to anything; there should never be a penalty for making an incorrect selection. The user can undo any selection by making any other selection.

How something is selected depends on what it is. Although there are many ways to select objects, they fall into easily recognizable groups. Users get used to selecting objects in a certain way, and applications that use these methods are easier to learn. Some of these methods apply to every type of application, and some only to particular types of applications.

Types of objects

Strictly speaking, *everything* on a Macintosh screen is displayed graphically. Still, it's useful to distinguish among three types of objects—text, graphics, and lists or arrays—because the user deals with each of them in a different way. Figure 3-52 shows an example of each.

```
The rest to some faint meaning make pretence
But Shadwell never deviates into sense.
Some beams of wit on other souls may fall,
Strike through and make a lucid interval;
But Shadwell's genuine night admits no ray,
His rising fogs prevail upon the day.


MacFlecknoe                    Page 1
```

Text

Advertising	132.9	
Manufacturing	121.3	
R & D	18.7	
Interest	12.2	
Total	285.1	

Array

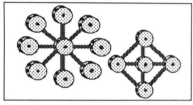

Graphics

Figure 3-52
Three ways of structuring information

Text can be arranged on the screen in a variety of ways. Some applications, such as word processors, might consist of nothing but text, whereas others, such as graphics-oriented applications, might use text almost incidentally. It's useful to consider all the text appearing together in a particular context as a block of text. The size of the block can range from a single field, as in a dialog box, to the whole document, as in a word processor. Regardless of its size or arrangement, the application sees each block as a one-dimensional string of characters. Text is edited the same way regardless of where it appears.

Arrays are one- or two-dimensional arrangements of **fields.** One-dimensional arrays are called **lists,** and two-dimensional arrays are called **tables** or **forms.** Each field, in turn, contains a collection of information, usually text, but possibly graphics. A table can be easily identified on the screen, because it consists of rows and columns of fields (sometimes called cells) separated by horizontal and vertical lines. A form is something the user fills out, like a tax form or credit-card application. The fields in a form can be arranged in any appropriate way; nevertheless, the application regards the fields as being in a definite linear order.

Graphics are pictures, drawn either by the user or by the application. Graphics in a document tend to (but do not have to) consist of discrete objects, each of which can be selected individually.

Each of these three ways of presenting information retains its integrity regardless of the context in which it appears. For example, a field in an array can contain text. When the user is manipulating the field as a whole, the field is treated as part of the array. When the user wants to change the contents of the field, he or she edits the field in the same way as any other text.

This section discusses first the general methods of selecting and then the specific methods that apply to text applications, graphics applications, and arrays.

Selection in general

This section covers the topic of selection without regard to the kind of data involved: selection by clicking, range selection, extending a selection, and discontinuous selection. In a monochrome environment, inverse video indicates what has been selected. Figure 3-53 compares some of the general methods.

Clicking on B selects B

Range selection of A through C
selects A, B, and C

Discontinuous selection
(range selection of A, B, and C
is extended to include E)

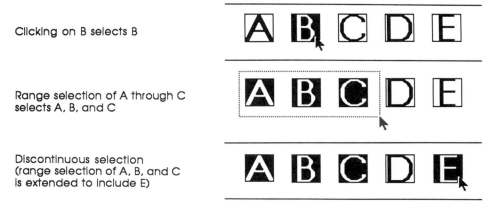

Figure 3-53
Selection methods

Selection by clicking

The most straightforward method of selecting an object is by clicking on it once. Icons, insertion points, and most other things that can be selected are selected this way.

Range selection

The user selects a range of objects by dragging through them. Although the exact meaning of the selection depends on the type of application, the procedure is always the same:

1. The user positions the pointer at one corner of the range and presses the mouse button. This position is called the **anchor point** of the range.

2. Without releasing the button, the user moves the pointer in any direction. As the pointer is moved, visual feedback indicates the objects that would be selected if the mouse button were released. For text and arrays, the selected area is continuously highlighted. For graphics, a dotted rectangle expands or contracts to show the range that will be selected. (If possible, the view should scroll to allow extending the selection beyond one windowful.)

3. When the feedback shows the desired range, the user releases the mouse button. The point at which the button is released is called the **active end** of the range.

Extending a selection

A user can change the extent of an existing selection by holding down the Shift key and clicking the mouse button (**Shift-click**). Exactly what happens next depends on the context.

In text or an array, the result of a Shift-click is always the selection of a range (Figure 3-54). The position where the button is clicked becomes the new endpoint of the range. If the user Shift-clicks *within* the current range, the new range will be smaller than the old range.

Extended selections can be made even across the panes of a split window.

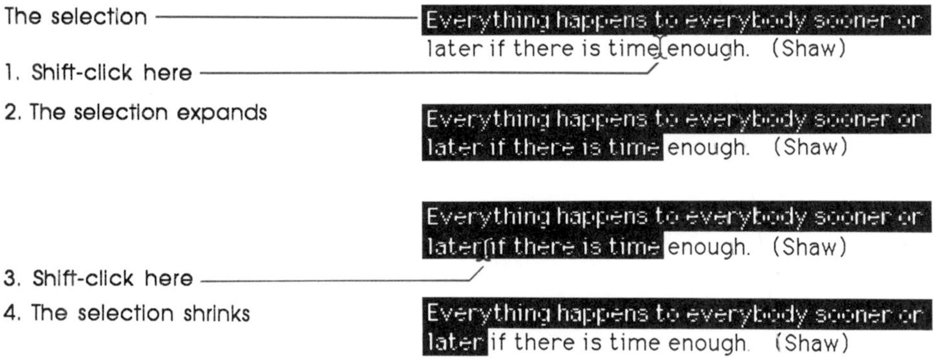

The selection ──────────── Everything happens to everybody sooner or later if there is time enough. (Shaw)

1. Shift-click here ───────────

2. The selection expands

Everything happens to everybody sooner or later if there is time enough. (Shaw)

Everything happens to everybody sooner or later if there is time enough. (Shaw)

3. Shift-click here ───────────
4. The selection shrinks

Everything happens to everybody sooner or later if there is time enough. (Shaw)

Figure 3-54
Expanding and shrinking a text selection

Making a discontinuous selection

In graphics applications, objects aren't usually considered to be in any particular sequence. A selection is extended by adding objects to it, and the added objects do not have to be adjacent to the objects already selected. The user can add either an individual object or a range of objects to the selection by holding down the Shift key before making the additional selection (Shift-click). When the user does this, the objects between the current selection and the new object are not automatically included in the selection. This kind of selection is called a **discontinuous selection.** If the user holds down the Shift key and selects one or more objects that are already highlighted, the objects are deselected.

In the case of graphics, all selections are discontinuous selections because graphic objects are discrete. This is not the case with arrays and text, in which an extended selection made by a Shift-click always includes everything between the old anchor point and the new endpoint. In arrays and text, discontinuous selections are made by clicking while holding down the Apple (Command) key.

To make a discontinuous selection in a text or array application, the user selects the first piece in the usual way and holds down the Apple key while selecting the remaining pieces. Each piece is selected in the same way as if it were the whole selection, but because the Apple key is held down, the new pieces are *added to* the existing selection instead of replacing it. If one of the pieces selected with Apple-click is already within an existing part of the selection, then instead of being added to the selection it's removed from the selection. Figure 3-55 shows a sequence in which several pieces are selected and deselected.

1. Cells B2, B3, C2, and C3 are selected

2. The user holds down the Apple key and clicks in D5

3. The user holds down the Apple key and clicks in C3

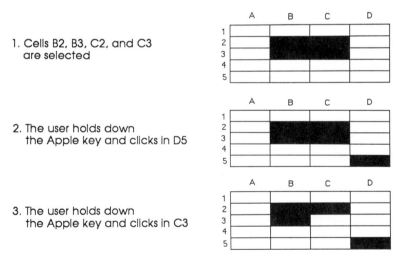

Figure 3-55
Discontinuous selection within an array

Not all applications support discontinuous selections, and those that do might restrict the operations a user can perform on them. For example, a word processor might allow the user to choose a font after making a discontinuous selection, but wouldn't allow the user to type replacement characters (which part of the selection would they replace?).

Selection by data type

This section covers the topic of selection according to the *kind* of data involved: text, graphics, and arrays.

Selections in text

In most applications, the user is required at some point to edit text. The principle of consistency (both within and among applications) requires that text be selected and edited in a consistent way, regardless of where it appears.

A block of text is a string of characters. A text selection is a substring of this string, which can have any length from zero characters to the whole block. Each of the text selection methods selects a different kind of substring. Figure 3-56 shows different kinds of text selections.

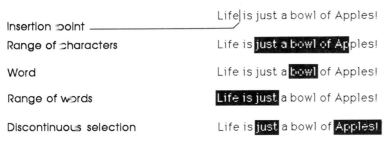

Insertion point — Life|is just a bowl of Apples!

Range of characters — Life is just a bowl of Apples!

Word — Life is just a bowl of Apples!

Range of words — Life is just a bowl of Apples!

Discontinuous selection — Life is just a bowl of Apples!

Figure 3-56
Text selections

The **insertion point** is a zero-length text selection. The user establishes the location of the insertion point by clicking somewhere in the text. The insertion point then appears at the nearest character boundary. If the user clicks anywhere to the right of the last character on a line, the insertion point appears immediately after the last character. If the user clicks to the left of the first character on a line, the insertion point appears immediately before the first character (unless the document is filled with space characters).

The insertion point shows where text will be inserted when the user begins typing, or where cut or copied data (the contents of the Clipboard) will be pasted. As each character is typed, it is inserted to the left of the insertion point.

If, between mouse-down (the moment the mouse button is pressed) and mouse-up (the moment the button is released), the user drags (moves the pointer more than about half the width of a character), the characters that were dragged across become selected. The selection is a range selection rather than an insertion point.

The user selects a whole word by double-clicking somewhere within that word. If the user begins a double-click sequence, but then drags the mouse between the mouse-down and the mouse-up of the second click, the selection becomes a range of words rather than a single word. As the pointer moves, the application highlights or unhighlights a whole word at a time.

A word or range of words can also be selected in the same way as any other range; whether this type of selection is treated as a range of characters or as a range of words depends on the operation. For example, in MacWrite, a range of individual characters that happens to coincide with a range of words is treated like characters for purposes of extending a selection, but is treated like words for purposes of "intelligent cut and paste" (described later in this chapter under "Editing Text").

The following definition of a *word* applies in the United States and Canada. In other countries, the definition differs to reflect local formats for numbers, dates, and currency. A word is defined as any continuous string that contains only the following characters:

- □ a letter
- □ a digit
- □ a nonbreaking space (Option-space or Apple-space)
- □ a currency symbol ($, ¢, £, or ¥)
- □ a percent sign
- □ a comma between digits
- □ a period before a digit
- □ an apostrophe between letters or digits
- □ a hyphen, but not a minus sign (Option-hyphen) or a dash (Option-Shift-hyphen)

If the user double-clicks over any character *not* on the list above, only that character is selected.

These are examples of words:

$123,456.78

shouldn't

3 1/2 (with a nonbreaking space)

.5%

These are examples of strings treated as more than one word:

7/10/6

blue cheese (with a breaking space)

"Wow!" (The quotation marks and exclamation point aren't part of the word.)

In some contexts—in a programming language, for example—it may be appropriate to allow users to select both the left and right parentheses in a pair, as well as all the characters between them, by double-clicking on either one of them. The same feature could be implemented for both braces and brackets. This would mean that the user could select the entire expression

[*x*+*y*-(4*3)^(*n*-1)]

simply by double-clicking on [or].

The user selects a range of text by dragging through the range. A range can be a range of characters, words, lines, or paragraphs, as defined by the application.

If the user extends the range, the way the range is extended depends on what kind of range it is. If it's a range of individual characters, it can be extended one character at a time. If it's a range of words (including a single word), it's extended only by whole words.

Making a selection with arrow keys

To use arrow keys to make a text selection, the user holds down Shift while pressing an arrow key. If it's important that your Macintosh application makes use of the numeric keypad, you shouldn't use these Shift-arrow key combinations. This is because the key codes for the four Shift-arrow key combinations are the same as those for the keypad's +, *, /, and = keys. If the use of a Shift-arrow key combination for making selections is more important to your application than is the numeric keypad, the following paragraphs describe how it should work.

When a Shift-arrow key combination is pressed, the active end of the selection moves and the range over which it moves becomes selected. If both the Shift key and another modifier key are held down, the end of the selection moves as defined for the particular modifier key, and the range over which it moves becomes selected. For example, Option-Shift-Left Arrow selects the whole word that contains the character to the left of the insertion point (just like double-clicking on a word).

A selection made by using the mouse is no different from one made by using arrow keys. A selection started with the mouse can be extended by using Shift and Left or Right Arrow.

In a text application, pressing Shift and either Left Arrow or Right Arrow selects a single character. Assuming that the Left Arrow key was used, the anchor point of the selection is on the right side of the selection, the active end on the left. Each subsequent Shift-Left Arrow adds another character to the left side of the selection. A Shift-Right Arrow at this point shrinks the selection. Figure 3-57 summarizes these actions.

1. Insertion point is within a word	word
2. Shift-← is pressed	w█rd
3. Another Shift-←	██rd
4. Shift-→	w█rd
5. Three more times Shift-→	wo██

Figure 3-57
Selecting with Shift and arrow keys

Pressing Option-Shift and either Left Arrow or Right Arrow (in a text application) selects the entire word containing the character to the left of the insertion point. Assuming Left Arrow was pressed, the anchor point is at the right end of the word, the active end at the left. Each subsequent Option-Shift-Left Arrow adds another word to the left end of the selection, as shown in Figure 3-58.

1. Insertion point is within a word	another word
2. Option-Shift-← is pressed	another █████
3. Another Option-Shift-←	█████████████

Figure 3-58
Selecting with Option-Shift and arrow keys

Undoing a text selection

When a block of text is selected, either with a pointing device or with cursor keys, pressing either Left Arrow or Right Arrow deselects the range. If Left Arrow is pressed, the insertion point goes to the beginning of what had been the selection. If Right Arrow is pressed, the insertion point goes to the end of what had been the selection.

Selections in graphics

In existing applications, there are several different ways to select graphic objects and to show selection feedback. This section shows how MacDraw and MacPaint do it, but other situations may require other solutions.

A MacDraw document is a collection of individual graphic objects. To select one of these objects, the user clicks once on the object, which is then bracketed with "handles." (The handles are used to stretch or shrink the object.) Figures 3-59 and 3-60 show examples of selection in MacDraw and MacPaint.

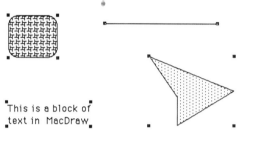

Figure 3-59
Graphic selection in MacDraw

In MacDraw, there are two ways to select more than one object. A range selection includes every object completely contained within the dotted rectangle that encloses the range as the user drags the mouse. A discontinuous selection includes only those objects explicitly selected.

A MacPaint document, on the other hand, is a series of pixels—not discrete objects. Selections are shown surrounded by a moving dashed line (sometimes called a marquee or "marching ants").

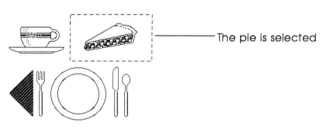

Figure 3-60
Graphic selection in MacPaint

Selections in arrays and tables

An array is a one- or two-dimensional arrangement of fields. The user can select one or more fields, or part of the contents of a field.

To select a single field, the user clicks in the field (Figure 3-61). The user can also select a field by moving into it with the Tab or Return key.

Click here to select Hawaii field ⎯

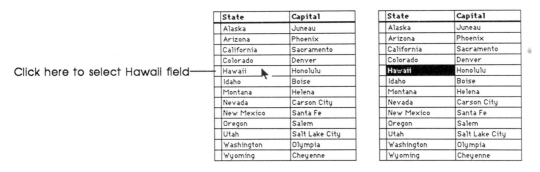

Figure 3-61
Field selection in an array

To select part of the contents of a field, the user must first select the field. The user then clicks again to select the desired part of the field. Because the contents of a field are either text or graphics, this type of selection follows the rules outlined above.

A table can also support selection of rows and columns. The most convenient way for the user to select a column is to click in the column header. To select more than one column, the user drags through several column headers. The same applies to rows.

Figures 3-62, 3-63, and 3-64 show column, range, and discontinuous selections in arrays.

Pressing the Tab key cycles the insertion point through the fields in an order determined by the application. From each field, the Tab key selects the "next" field. Typically, the sequence of fields is first from left to right, and then from top to bottom. When the last field in a form is selected, pressing the Tab key selects the first field in the form. If there's a good reason, an application may guide the user through the fields in some order other than the order in which the fields appear on the screen.

The Return key selects the first field in the next row. If the idea of rows doesn't make sense in a particular context, then the Return key should have the same effect as the Tab key.

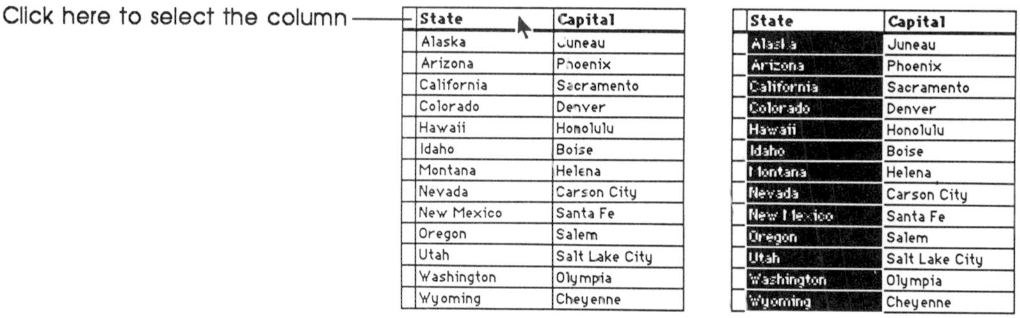

Click here to select the column ———

State	Capital
Alaska	Juneau
Arizona	Phoenix
California	Sacramento
Colorado	Denver
Hawaii	Honolulu
Idaho	Boise
Montana	Helena
Nevada	Carson City
New Mexico	Santa Fe
Oregon	Salem
Utah	Salt Lake City
Washington	Olympia
Wyoming	Cheyenne

State	Capital
Alaska	Juneau
Arizona	Phoenix
California	Sacramento
Colorado	Denver
Hawaii	Honolulu
Idaho	Boise
Montana	Helena
Nevada	Carson City
New Mexico	Santa Fe
Oregon	Salem
Utah	Salt Lake City
Washington	Olympia
Wyoming	Cheyenne

Figure 3-62
Column selection in an array

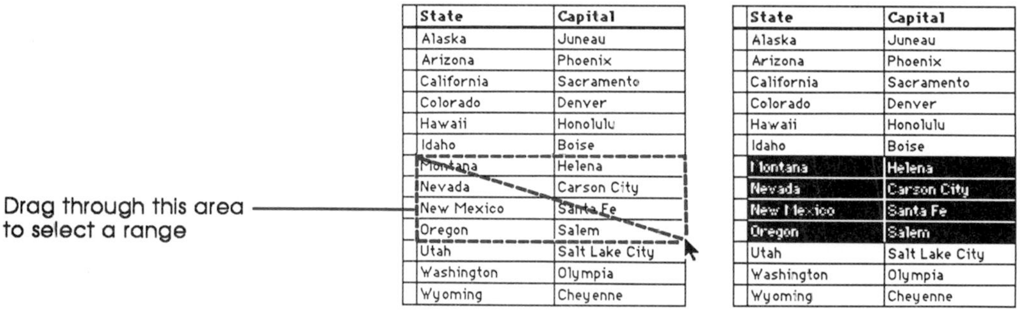

State	Capital
Alaska	Juneau
Arizona	Phoenix
California	Sacramento
Colorado	Denver
Hawaii	Honolulu
Idaho	Boise
Montana	Helena
Nevada	Carson City
New Mexico	Santa Fe
Oregon	Salem
Utah	Salt Lake City
Washington	Olympia
Wyoming	Cheyenne

Drag through this area ———
to select a range

State	Capital
Alaska	Juneau
Arizona	Phoenix
California	Sacramento
Colorado	Denver
Hawaii	Honolulu
Idaho	Boise
Montana	Helena
Nevada	Carson City
New Mexico	Santa Fe
Oregon	Salem
Utah	Salt Lake City
Washington	Olympia
Wyoming	Cheyenne

Figure 3-63
Range selection in an array

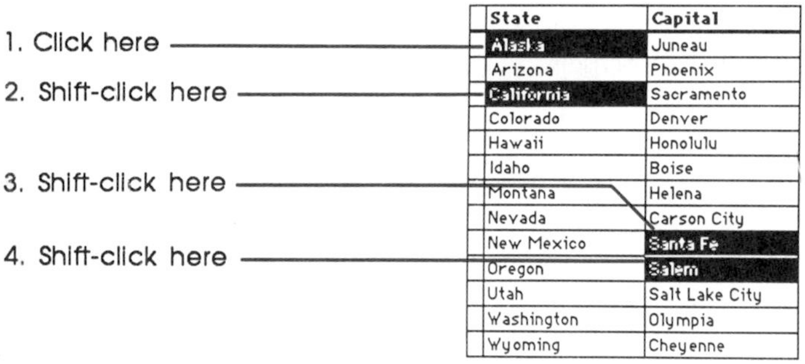

1. Click here ———
2. Shift-click here ———
3. Shift-click here ———
4. Shift-click here ———

State	Capital
Alaska	Juneau
Arizona	Phoenix
California	Sacramento
Colorado	Denver
Hawaii	Honolulu
Idaho	Boise
Montana	Helena
Nevada	Carson City
New Mexico	Santa Fe
Oregon	Salem
Utah	Salt Lake City
Washington	Olympia
Wyoming	Cheyenne

Figure 3-64
Discontinuous selection in an array

Editing text

In addition to the editing features that the user accesses through the Edit menu, there are ways to edit text without using menu commands.

Inserting text

To insert text, the user selects an insertion point by clicking where the text is to go, then starts typing. The application continually moves the insertion point to the right as each new character is added.

Applications with multiple-line text blocks should support **word wraparound.** That is, no word should be broken between lines.

Backspacing

When the user presses the Backspace or Delete key, one of two things happens:

- If the current selection is an insertion point, the character to the left of the insertion point is deleted.
- If the current selection is one or more characters, it's deleted. (This is equivalent to choosing Clear from the Edit menu.)

In either case, the insertion point replaces the deleted character (or characters) in the document. The deleted characters don't go into the Clipboard, but the user can undo the deletion by immediately choosing Undo.

Replacing text

If the user starts typing when the selection is one or more characters, the characters that are typed replace the selection. The deleted characters don't go into the Clipboard, but the user can undo the replacement by immediately choosing Undo.

Intelligent cut and paste

"Intelligent" cut and paste is a set of editing features that takes into account the need for spaces between words. To understand why this feature is helpful, consider the following sequence of events in a text application *without* intelligent cut and paste:

1. A sentence in the user's document reads

   Returns are only accepted if the merchandise is damaged.

   The user wants to change this to

   Returns are accepted only if the merchandise is damaged.

2. The user selects the word *only* by double-clicking. The letters are highlighted, but neither of the adjacent spaces is highlighted.

3. The user chooses Cut, clicks just before the word *if,* and chooses Paste.

4. The sentence now reads

   Returns are accepted onlyif the merchandise is damaged.

   Note the extra space between *are* and *accepted,* and the lack of a space between *only* and *if.* To correct the sentence, the user has to remove the extra space between *are* and *accepted,* and add one between *only* and *if.* At this point he or she may be wondering why people bother with computers at all.

If an application supports intelligent cut and paste, these are the rules:

☐ If the user selects a word or a range of words, the selection itself is highlighted, but spaces adjacent to the selection are not highlighted.

☐ When the user chooses Cut, if the character to the left of the selection is a space, cut the space along with the selection. If the character to the left of the selection is not a space, but the character to the right of the selection is a space, cut that space along with the selection.

☐ When the user chooses Paste, if the character to the left or right of the current selection is part of a word, insert a space before pasting.

If the left or right end of a text selection is a word, follow these rules at that end, regardless of whether there's a word at the other end. Figure 3-65 shows two examples of intelligent cut and paste.

1. Select a word	Drink to me ▓only▓ with thine eyes.
2. Choose Cut	Drink to me| with thine eyes.
3. Select an insertion point	Drink to me with |thine eyes.
4. Choose Paste	Drink to me with only|thine eyes.

1. Select a word	How, ▓now▓ brown cow
2. Choose Cut	How,| brown cow
3. Select an insertion point	How|, brown cow
4. Choose Paste	How now|, brown cow

Figure 3-65
Intelligent cut and paste

Note that the selected text is not necessarily exactly the same range that will be cut and, eventually, pasted.

Intelligent cut and paste should be used only if the application supports the full definition of a word (as detailed in this chapter under "Selections in Text"), rather than the definition of a word as "anything between two spaces." These rules apply to any selection consisting of one or more whole words, whether the user selected it with a double click or as a range selection.

Editing fields

If an application isn't primarily a text application, but does use text in fields (such as in a dialog box), you may not need to provide the full text-editing capabilities described so far. In Macintosh applications, the simplest way to implement text editing is to use TextEdit in the User Interface Toolbox. It's important, however, that whatever editing capabilities the application provides under these circumstances be upward-compatible with the full text-editing capabilities. The following list ranks the capabilities that can be provided, in a continuum from the minimum set to the most sophisticated features:

☐ The user can select the whole field and type in a new value, use backspace, select a substring of the field and replace it, and select a word by double-clicking.

☐ The user can choose Undo, Cut, Copy, Paste, and Clear, as described in this chapter under "The Edit Menu."

☐ Intelligent cut and paste is fully implemented. (TextEdit does not provide this.)

Even applications with only minimal text editing should perform appropriate edit checks. For example, if the only legitimate value for a field is a string of digits, the application should issue an alert message if the user types any nondigits. For example, the alert message might interrupt the erring user to remind him or her that the letters *l* and *O* can't be used in place of the numerals *1* and *0*. Alternatively, the application could wait until the user is through typing before checking the validity of a field's contents. In this case, the appropriate time to check the field is when the user clicks anywhere other than within the field or presses the Return, Enter, or Tab key.

Appendix A

The Roots of the Apple Desktop Interface

The Apple employees who created the Apple Desktop Interface had been involved in, or were influenced by, important research done at several institutions over the previous twenty or more years.

In the early 1960s, the Augmentation Research Project at SRI International made important contributions. Its focus was the "augmentation of human intellect." This notion put the human being, rather than technology, at the center of human-computer interactions and resulted in some unique concepts of what a human interface should be. Most directly, it implied that the goal of human-computer interactions was the enhancement of human performance, in contrast to other contemporary efforts that focused either on technology development in isolation, or on the development of control panels that helped people "keep up with" and guide powerful computational systems.

This augmentation approach led to hardware innovations, the principal example of which is the mouse, which lets people drive computer interactions by pointing at the screen rather than typing commands at the keyboard. This approach is a central tenet of the Apple Desktop Interface.

Important work at Xerox Corporation's Palo Alto Research Center (Xerox PARC) extended the concept of humans at the center of human-computer interactions. In the early 1970s, PARC provided the first explicit expression of the computer desktop. PARC's desktop featured windows that overlap on the screen, much like overlapping pieces of paper on a real desktop. Icons, typically representing familiar objects, appeared on the desktop to provide direct and visible access to files, operations, and so on. Bit-mapped graphics enabled users to directly combine text and graphics.

At Apple in the late 1970s and early 1980s, the development of the Lisa computer carried the work still further. A range of features now familiar in the Apple Desktop Interface—including the menu bar, the one-button mouse, dialog boxes, the Clipboard, and the trash can—were introduced with the Lisa. This palette of consistent elements made Lisa very easy to learn and use.

The Apple Macintosh computer made these human interface features more approachable and available on a less expensive machine, again emphasizing the humanness of the machine and the computer's role as a tool for magnifying human capability.

The Apple Desktop Interface can be implemented to some degree on any Apple computer. The goal is to provide a consistent interface for users of many machines, so that users can take advantage of the unique features of each machine within the context of a familiar and approachable interface.

Appendix B

Software for International Markets

General guidelines

Localization is the process of adapting an application to a specific locale. By making localization relatively painless, you'll ensure that international markets are available for your product in the future. You'll also allow English-speaking users in other countries to buy the U.S. English version of your software and use it, if they wish to, with their native languages. To create easily localized software, you must follow certain guidelines for the use of text, fonts, sorting, and date/time display.

- ☐ Make quoted strings that will have to be translated easy for the translator to find. No text the user sees should be in the program code itself. Storing user-visible text in resources will make translation easier.

- ☐ If your program relies on properties of the ASCII code table or uses data compression codes that assume a certain number of letters in the alphabet, remember that not all alphabets have the same numbers of characters. German, for example, has 30 characters, English 26.

- ☐ Don't assume that all languages have the same rules for punctuation, word order, and alphabetizing. In Spanish, questions both begin and end with a question mark—the beginning one being an upside-down version of the closing one. The roles of commas and periods in numbers is sometimes the reverse of what you may be used to—in many countries the number 3,546.98 is rendered 3.546,98.

- ☐ Don't let your program rely on strings having a particular length. Translation will make most strings longer.

- Laws and customs vary. The elements of addresses don't always appear in the same order. In some countries, the postal zone code precedes the name of the city, in other countries it's the reverse. Postal zone codes don't contain the same number of characters in every country, and in some countries they contain letters as well as numbers. The rules for amortizing mortgages and calculating interest rates vary from country to country—even between Canada and the United States.

- Keyboards vary from country to country. Some characters appear on some keyboards and not on others. Keystrokes that are easily performed with one hand in your own country may require two hands in another. In France and Italy, for example, typing numerals requires pressing the Shift key.

- Units of measure and standard formats for time and date differ from country to country. For example, "lines per inch" is meaningless in the metric world—that is, almost everywhere. In some countries, the 24-hour clock prevails. Such culture-dependent information can be read from resources so that the application automatically works correctly in countries where those resources have been properly set up.

- Words aren't the only things that change from country to country. Telephones and mailboxes, to name just two examples often used in telecommunications programs, don't look the same in all parts of the world. Either make your graphics culturally neutral, or be prepared to create alternate graphics for various cultures.

- Mnemonic shortcuts that are valid in one language may not be valid in others. Make sure all such shortcuts are also in resources.

Macintosh localization

This section is specific to the Macintosh family of computers. For full details, see *Inside Macintosh.*

The Macintosh Resource Manager allows the separation of code and data. Data (in the form of resources) can be edited with a number of tools such as REdit and ResEdit. Changing the appropriate resources lets you change the appearance of an application (dialog boxes, messages, menus, and so on) without rebuilding the application code. Always use the Macintosh's international resources where applicable.

Text

For legibility, some non-Roman characters need higher resolution than Roman characters. On the Japanese Macintosh Plus, for example, the system font must be larger than normal—it must allow for 16-by-16 pixel characters. The Macintosh Plus ROM sets the system font size and family according to low-memory variables. For example, it is possible to specify text in dialog boxes and menu bars to 14-point New York. Applications should not change the system font or font size: let the user (or the system, where that is possible) make such changes. Applications can use SysFontSize to get the default font size to use for their text.

Line spacing

Most Roman fonts for the Macintosh have space above all the letters to allow for diacritical marks as with Ä or Ñ. If text is drawn using a standard font immediately below a dark line, for example, it will appear to be separated from the line by at least one row of blank pixels (for all but a few exceptional characters). Pixels in some non-Roman fonts, on the other hand, can extend to the top of the character, and appear to merge with the preceding line. To avoid character display overlap, applications should leave blank space around text (as in dialog editText items) or add space *before* the first line of text and *after* the last line of text, as well as *between* lines of text.

Font selection

The choice of script (or alphabet: Roman, Kanji, Arabic, and so on) depends on the fonts chosen by the user. If an application does not allow the user to change fonts, or allows the user only to select a global font for the whole document, then the user is restricted in the choice and mix of scripts.

Uppercase and lowercase

If text must be displayed in either uppercase or lowercase, the application should call the Transliterate routine (in the Script Manager) to perform the operation. The UprString routine in the Macintosh ROM is designed to be used by the File system and as such does not handle diacritical marks or non-Roman scripts correctly.

Menus

In the Macintosh Plus ROM, the Menu Manager uses the system font and the system font size in setting up the height of the menu bar, and of the items in menus. Because the system font size can vary, the height of the menu bar can also vary. When determining window placement on the screen, do not assume that the menu bar height is 20. Applications should use the low memory variable MBarHeight (instead of 20) as the height of the menu bar.

If a menu contains too many items to display at once, on a Macintosh Plus the menu scrolls to reveal the hidden items. This feature was devised only for the menus to which the user can add many items—the Font menu specifically. Application programmers should not create menus that are too long to be seen without scrolling.

Applications should avoid using too many menus, because translation into other languages almost always widens menu titles, forcing some far to the right (possibly conflicting with the Switcher), or even off the screen. Applications should always leave room for the menu that some desk accessories add to the menu bar.

The International Utilities Package

The International Utilities Package provides routines for dealing with sorting, currency, measurement systems, and date and time formatting. It is important that you use the routines in this package, rather than the System Utility routines contained in the Macintosh ROM—the ROM routines are not as accurate and (because they are used by the File system) they can't be localized for different countries.

The Script Manager

The Script Manager contains routines that allow an application to function correctly with non-Roman scripts. It also contains utility routines for text processing and parsing, which are useful for applications that do a lot of text manipulation. General applications don't need to call Script Manager routines directly, but can be localized for non-Roman alphabets through such script interface systems as Apple's Kanji Interface System (KanjiTalk) and Arabic Interface System.

Dialog and alert boxes

Give text room to grow during localization. For example, don't create a screen-sized dialog box that is completely filled with text. Most languages require more characters than English does to convey equivalent messages.

When creating parameterized text, be sure the localizer will be able to rearrange the sentence as needed. For example, if an alert box sentence is to say

There was a problem doing ^0 to the ^1

then the localizer will be able to correctly order the noun and prepositional phrase for different languages.

Avoid hard-coding positions for drawing text or graphics. If possible, use a UserItem for positioning or dynamic display or PICT to display static graphics.

Appendix C

Recommended Reading

The following works are recommended for those interested in further reading on human interface design and the use of color.

Articles and Papers

☐ Baron, S., and R. W. Pew. "Perspectives on Human Performance Modelling." *Automatica,* November 1983, 663–676.

☐ Buxton, W. "A Directory of Sources for Interactive Technologies." *SIG-CHI Bulletin,* July 1986, 58–63.

☐ Carroll, John. "Presentation and Form in User-Interface Architecture." *BYTE,* December 1983, 113–122.

☐ Carroll, John, and Mary Beth Rosson. "Beyond MIPS*: Performance Is Not Quality." *BYTE,* February 1984, 168–172.

☐ Colby, K. M., L. Tesler, and H. Enea. "Experiments With a Search Algorithm for the Data Base of a Human Belief Structure." *Proceedings of the International Joint Conference on Artificial Intelligence,* May 1969, 649–654.

☐ Covington, Jon S. "The Uses of Apple in Training." *Society for Applied Learning Technology,* February 1983.

☐ Gassée, Jean-Louis. "The Next Decade: An Insider's View." *A+: The Independent Guide to Apple Computing,* February 1987, 51–53.

☐ Hooper, K. "A Cognitive Approach to Computer Graphics, Environmental Simulation and Design." *Proceedings of the International Conference on Cybernetics and Society,* 1975, 112–113.

☐ Kay, A. "Inventing the Future (Computer Industry)." In *AI Business. The Commercial Uses of Artificial Intelligence.* Cambridge, MA: MIT Press, 1984, 103-112.

☐ Kay, A. "Smaller Is More Portable." *Computing (GB),* June 1984, 28.

☐ Kay, A., and A. Goldberg. "Personal Dynamic Media." *Computer (USA),* March 1977, 31–41.

☐ Licklider, J. C., et al. "The Computer as a Communication Device." *International Science and Technology,* 76, 21–31.

☐ Miller, D.C., and R. W. Pew. "Exploiting User Involvement in Interactive System Development." *Proceedings of the Human Factors Society 25th Annual Meeting,* 1981, 401–405.

☐ Minsky, M. R. "Manipulating Simulated Objects with Real-World Gestures Using a Force and Position Sensitive Screen." *Comput. and Graphics (GB),* July 1984, 195–203.

☐ Myers, B.A., and W. Buxton. "Creating Highly-Interactive and Graphical User Interfaces by Demonstration." *Comput. Graphics (USA),* August 1986, 249–256.

☐ Price, Jonathan. "How Apple Put Training on a Disk." *Softalk,* July 1984, 48–55.

☐ Schneiderman, Ben. "Direct Manipulation: A Step Beyond Programming Languages." *IEEE Computer,* 16 (8), 57–69.

☐ Sculley, John. "Why We Need a Counterbalance." *Personal Computing,* October 1986, 280.

☐ Shackel, B. "Man-Computer Interaction: The Contribution of the Human Sciences." *IEEE Trans. Man-Mach. Syst. (USA),* December 1969, 149–163.

☐ Shackel, B. "Designing for People in the Age of Information." *Comput. Compacts (Netherlands),* 2 (5–6), 150–157.

☐ Shackel, B. "The Ergonomics of the Man-Computer Interface." *Infotech (GB),* 1979, 299–324.

☐ Smith, D. C., et al. "Designing the Star User Interface." *BYTE,* 7 (4), 242–282.

☐ Spiliotopoulos, V., and B. Shackel. "Towards a Computer Interview Acceptable to the Naive User." *Int. J. Man-Mach. Stud. (GB),* 14 (1), 77–90.

☐ Tesler, Larry. "Enlisting User Help in Software Design." *SIG-CHI Bulletin,* January 1983, 5–7.

☐ Tesler, Larry. "Object-Oriented User Interfaces and Object-Oriented Languages." *ACM Conference on Personal and Small Computers,* 1983, 3–5.

☐ Tesler, Larry. "The Legacy of the Lisa." *Macworld,* September 1985, 17–22. How the Lisa changed personal computing, by a member of the Lisa design team.

☐ Tesler, Larry. "Programming Experiences." *BYTE,* August 1986, 195.

Books

☐ Apple Computer, Inc. *Inside Macintosh.* Reading, MA: Addison-Wesley, 1985–1987, five volumes. The essential reference for Macintosh programmers. Chapters on memory management, assembly language, the Resource Manager, QuickDraw, the Font Manager, the Toolbox Event Manager, the Window Manager, the Control Manager, and so on. Note that the "User Interface Guidelines" chapter in *Inside Macintosh* is superseded by *Human Interface Guidelines: The Apple Desktop Interface.*

☐ Baecker, Ron, and William Buxton, eds. *Readings in Human-Computer Interaction: A Multidisciplinary Approach.* Des Moines, IA: Morgan Kaufmann, 1987.

☐ Beech, D., ed. *Concepts in User Interfaces. Lecture Notes in Computer Science Series,* vol. 234, New York: Springer-Verlag, 1986.

☐ Berryman, Gregg. *Notes on Graphic Design and Visual Communication.* Los Altos, CA: William Kaufmann, 1984. Deals with logos, colors, many other topics.

☐ Bertin, Jacques. *Semiology of Graphics.* Madison: University of Wisconsin Press, 1983.

☐ Bolt, Richard A. *The Human Interface: Where People and Computers Meet.* New York: Van Nostrand Reinhold, 1984.

☐ Card, Stuart K., et al. *The Psychology of Human-Computer Interaction.* Hillsdale, NJ: Lawrence Erlbaum Associates, 1983.

☐ Carroll, J. M. *Interfacing Thought: Cognitive Aspects of Human Computer Interaction.* Hillsdale, NJ: Lawrence Erlbaum Associates, 1987.

☐ Coombs, M. J., and J. L. Alty. *Computing Skills and the User Interface*. New York: Academic Press, 1981.

☐ Diethelm, Walter. *Signet Sign Symbol*. Zürich: ABC Verlag, 1976.

☐ Drexler, Eric. *Engines of Creation*. New York: Doubleday, 1986. Foreword by Marvin Minsky.

☐ Dreyfuss, Henry. *Symbol Sourcebook, an Authoritative Guide to International Graphic Symbols*. New York: Van Nostrand Reinhold, 1984. Foreword by R. Buckminster Fuller. Symbols are grouped by subject areas. Includes index.

☐ Engelbart, Douglas C. *Augmenting Human Intellect, a Conceptual Framework*. Menlo Park, CA: Stanford Research Institute, 1962.

☐ Favre, Jean-Paul, and André November. *Color and Communication*. Zürich: ABC Verlag, 1979.

☐ Frutiger, Adrian. *Type Sign Symbol*. Zürich: ABC Verlag, 1980.

☐ Gassée, Jean-Louis. *The Third Apple: Personal Computers and the Cultural Revolution*. New York: Harcourt Brace Jovanovich, 1987.

☐ Goldberg, A. *Smalltalk-80, the Interactive Programming Environment*. Reading, MA: Addison-Wesley, 1984.

☐ Green, Thomas, and Ernest Edmonds, eds. *The Ergonomics of the User Interface. Behaviour and Information Technology Special Issue Series,* vol. 3, no. 2. Philadelphia: Taylor & Francis, 1984.

☐ Greenberg, D., A. Marcus, A. Schmidt, and V. Gorter. *The Computer Image*. Menlo Park, CA: Addison-Wesley, 1982.

☐ Guedj, R. A., et al. *Methodology of Interaction*. Amsterdam: North-Holland, 1980.

☐ Heckel, Paul. *The Elements of Friendly Software Design*. New York: Warner Books, 1984.

☐ Hildreth, Charles. Foreword by C. Lee Jones. *Online Public Access Catalogs: The User Interface. OCLC Library Information and Computer Science Series*. Dublin, OH: OCLC Online Comp, 1982.

☐ Hunt, Morton. *The Universe Within*. New York: Simon & Schuster, 1982.

☐ Itten, Johannes. *The Elements of Color,* edited by F. Birren. New York: Van Nostrand Reinhold, 1970.

☐ Kay, Alan. *Creative Art Through Photography*. Newton Centre, MA: Branford, 1973.

☐ Kay, Alan. *My Generations*. New York: Behrman, 1984.

☐ Lindsay, Peter H., and Donald A. Norman. *Human Information Processing: An Introduction to Psychology*. New York: Academic Press, 1977.

☐ McConnell, Vicki. *Building the End User Interface*. Reading, MA: Addison-Wesley, 1983.

☐ McCormick, Ernest J. *Human Factors in Engineering and Design*. New York: McGraw-Hill, 1976.

☐ McKim, Robert H. *Experiences in Visual Thinking*. Monterey, CA: Brooks/Cole, 1972.

☐ Minsky, Marvin. *Computation: Finite and Infinite Machines*. Englewood Cliffs, NJ: Prentice-Hall, 1967.

☐ Minsky, Marvin. *The Society of Mind*. New York: Simon & Schuster, 1987.

☐ Modley, Rudolf. *Handbook of Pictorial Symbols*. New York: Dover Publications, 1976.

☐ Nelson, Theodor H. *Computer Lib*. Schooleys Mountain, NJ: Nelson, 1974.

☐ Nelson, Theodor H. *Literary Machines*. Schooleys Mountain, NJ: Nelson, 1981.

☐ Nickerson, Raymond S. *Using Computers. Human Factors in Information Systems*. Cambridge, MA: MIT Press, 1986.

☐ Norman, Donald A. *Memory and Attention: An Introduction to Human Information Processing*. New York: Wiley, 1976.

☐ Norman, Donald A., ed. *Perspectives on Cognitive Science*. Hillsdale, NJ: Lawrence Erlbaum Associates, 1981.

☐ Norman, Donald A., ed. *Perspectives on Cognitive Science*. Norwood, NJ: Ablex, 1981.

☐ Norman, Donald A. *Learning and Memory*. San Francisco: W. H. Freeman, 1982.

☐ Norman, Donald A. *The Psychology of Everyday Things*. New York: Basic Books, 1988.

☐ Norman, Donald A., and Stephen Draper, eds. *User Centered System Design*. Hillsdale, NJ: Lawrence Erlbaum Associates, 1986. Compilation of articles by nineteen authors.

☐ Norman, Donald A., and David E. Rumelhart. *Explorations in Cognition*. San Francisco: W. H. Freeman, 1975.

☐ Pfaff, G., ed. *User Interface Management Systems*. New York: Springer-Verlag, 1985.

☐ Schneiderman, Ben, ed. *Data Bases: Improving Usability and Effectiveness*. New York: Academic Press, 1978.

☐ Schneiderman, Ben. *Software Psychology: Human Factors in Computer and Information Systems*. Cambridge, MA: Winthrop Publishers, 1980.

☐ Schneiderman, Ben. *Designing the User Interface: Strategies for Effective Human-Computer Interaction*. Reading, MA: Addison-Wesley, 1987.

☐ Simpson, H. K. *Programming the Macintosh User Interface*. New York: McGraw-Hill, 1986.

☐ Smith, H. T., and T. R. G. Green, eds. *Human Interaction with Computers*. New York: Academic Press, 1980.

☐ Vassilou, Y. *Human Factors and Interactive Computer Systems*. Norwood, NJ: Ablex, 1982.

☐ Whitney, Patrick, and Cheryl Kent, eds. *Design in the Information Environment*. New York: Knopf, 1985.

Periodicals

☐ *Cognitive Science*. Journal of the Cognitive Science Society.

☐ *Ergonomics*. Published by the Ergonomics Research Society, London, quarterly since 1957, monthly since 1982.

☐ "Human Factors in Computing Systems," annual issue of the *SIG-CHI Bulletin,* the journal of ACM's SIG-CHI (the Association for Computing Machinery's Special Interest Group on Computers and Human Interaction). Once a year, the Bulletin is devoted to the proceedings of SIG-CHI's annual meeting.

☐ *Human Factors: the Journal of the Human Factors Society*. Santa Monica, California. Published since September 1958.

☐ *Human Factors Review*. Published by the Human Factors Society, Santa Monica, California. Published since 1985.

☐ *IEEE Transactions on Systems, Man, and Cybernetics*.

☐ *International Journal of Man-Machine Studies*.

☐ *Proceedings of the Annual Conference of Cognitive Science Society*.

Index

in arrays 116–117
arrow keys and 113–114
by clicking 108
color and 35
by data type 111–117
discontinuous 109–111
extending or shrinking 109
in graphics 115–117
in MacDraw 115
in MacPaint 115
methods of 108–117
by range 109, 111–113
scrolling after 52
in text 111–114
undoing 29, 99, 109–111, 119
visual cues for 29
semantic modifier 104
serifs 84
settings, changing. *See* controls
Shadow command (Style
menu) 68, 69, 86
shapes, pointer 28–29
Shift-arrow key 113–114
Shift-click 109
Shift key 12, 30, 72, 100, 102,
109, 113–114
short-term modes 12
Show Clipboard command (Edit
menu) 81, 84
Show Rulers command (Format
menu) 68
size box 22–23, 42–43, 44–45
Size menu. *See* FontSize menu
small caps 86
snapshot, screen 101
software. *See* applications
sound 17, 36–37
spatial orientation 4, 6
special characters 69, 100
Special Education Programs,
Office of 16
specifications 39–121
spelling checkers 63, 74
spinning beachball pointer 29, 94,
95
split bars 53–54
split windows 42, 53–54
SRI International 123
stability, illusion of 8, 25, 40
stationery files 42

stationery icons 41, 78–79
Stationery option 78–79
status indicator 95
stop alert 61
strings 125–126
Style menu 56, 68, 69, 73, 74, 86
Bold command 68, 69, 73, 86
Italic command 68, 69, 86
keyboard equivalents and 73
Outline command 68, 69
Plain Text command 68, 86, 73
Shadow command 68, 69, 86
text styles in 69
Underline command 66, 68, 69,
73, 86
styluses 28
submenu delay 87
submenus. *See* hierarchical menus
subscript 86
superscript 86
symbol keys 100
SysFontSize 127
System file 74
system font 127

T

Tab key 82, 98, 116
tables 107, 116–117
tear-off menus 91–92
Technical Publications Group (Apple
Computer, Inc.) xii
templates. *See* stationery files
testing 15–16, 37
text
arranging 107
color 34, 35
editing 118–121
enlarged 16
entering 12, 27, 30, 98
inserting 118
printing 6
replacing 118
scrolling 12
selecting 12, 111–114
TextEdit resource 120
text fields 58, 61
title bar 22–23, 42–43, 44–45, 46
color and 35

toggled menu items 56, 68, 81,
84, 86
Toolbox, controls and 56
tools, ROM-based 11, 46, 127–128
track balls 28
training materials, color and 35
translation 42, 125
Transliterate routine (Script
Manager) 127
Trash icon 5, 22, 41, 42, 124
triple-clicking (mouse
technique) 96
tutorial materials, color and 35
type-ahead 101
typeface. *See* font(s)
typographical characters 84

U

Underline command (Style
menu) 66, 68, 69, 73, 86
underline mode 12
Undo command (Edit menu) 27,
29, 80–81, 82
function of 82
keyboard equivalent for 72–73
operations that can't be
undone 82
toggled 68
undoing selections 29, 99,
109–111, 119
units, international differences 126
Up Arrow key 102
uppercase letters 30, 67, 72, 86,
100, 127
UprString routine (Macintosh
ROM) 127
User Interface Toolbox, TextEdit
resource in 120
user control 7
of color 33
of sound 37
users 4
disabled 16–17
model of 2–3
user testing 15–16, 37
utilities 63. *See also specific utility*